HOPE FOR THE FAMILY

MOSES PLANGKAT

First Published in April 2022

ISBN: 978-93-5611-386-2

BLUEROSE PUBLISHERS

www.bluerosepublishers.com

info@bluerosepublishers.com

+91 8882 898 898

Cover Design:

Muskan Sachdeva

Typographic Design:

Sachvesh

Distributed by: BlueRose, Amazon, Flipkart

Dedication

I dedicate this book to God who gives wisdom and direction; and most importantly to every family around the globe.

Foreword

It would be obvious for an adult, who may have married and experienced family life or who may have watched married persons struggle with marital issues, to launch out to write on the subject matter. For a young single adult that the author is to do so underscores the need for revisiting the family in the wake of increasingly low social and moral values among the youths. The author has addressed issues such as who a child is and what it takes to guide him/her to grow into a responsible husband and father or wife and mother. The book has been presented in convenient bits for ease of reference. Parenting has been given prominence as a key factor in child upbringing. The role of the teacher, at both formal and informal and/or religious levels has not been neglected. These pieces of writing have been beefed up with biblical examples of outstanding children that were influenced by godly parents.

I recommend the four-part book titled HOPE FOR THE FAMILY to young people aspiring for marriage, married couples – whether just married or old in marriage, grand parents, school teachers, religious instructors, social workers, administrators and all who may have anything to do with youths. The author has not only identified problems but has pointed the way forward, by referring readers to the Author and Finisher of life. In Him we all exist and have our being.

Oliver N. Ndam (Ph.D.)

National Chairman (FCS) and Marriage Counselor

Acknowledgement

Firstly, I want to thank God for giving me the opportunity, and guiding me through the whole project. He actually was my highest motivation towards making this book a success, irrespective of all the challenges faced, He was there.

To my Parents and family Mr. and Mrs. Moses Dashal, Mr. Longji Moses and Family, Mr. Jephter Yamchan and family, Mr. Zugumnan Moses. To Dr. Daniel Gobgab and family, Mrs. Gloria Ret, Mr. Nanbal Ladan and family, you are a source of encouragement when my strength was failing and for guidance all through. Dr. Oliver Ndam, you are another figure that came at the tail end of the journey or project to give it a new look, the editing work and contribution cannot be emphasized, also Mrs. Blessing Sainaan Lagan who also made sacrifice to edit the whole work. I want to specially thank the Sunday School Unit of COCIN Bukuru Gyel and Children's Unit of God Life Assembly International (Jos) for giving me the opportunity to serve and the inspiration towards making this book a huge success.

Mr. Jim, Mulapkat Chingyin, Mr. Lazarus Gyang, Miss. Abigail Malan, Mrs. Nayen Baget and Mr. Tochi Samuel thanks for contributing to the content. Most importantly, thank you very much to victims who were able to open up to share their life transforming stories to see that another child and family is been saved, thanks for being bold enough, I celebrate you really for my deepest heart.

To my friends: Jerry Nimyel, Nathaniel Izang, Fatgan Mercy Agati, Ayuba Ishaku, Janet Sati, Zion Ode and Lumi Ayuba, you are so amazing, kept in touch and the show of concern has been another inspiration I won't take for granted; and others whose name I cannot recall, just know that from my heart I really appreciate you for praying and encouraging me when needed it, having you around is worth it.

Finally, with deep sense of gratitude, without you, this book will not have been a success: Dr. Obed Ikwegbu for believing in me and working hard the best way you can all through; Mr. Nantok Tohomdet and Prof. Suleiman Bogoro and Hon. Pam Botmang, thanks for believing and supporting the project; Pastor Chingtok Ishaku and Rev. Dr. Obed Dashan for being spiritual parents in the course of this project, God bless you.

Preface

The system and tradition of parenting handed down to our generation have been a distorted/adulterated one. Some values that were practiced before are now no longer tenable. But those were the values that preserved the generations of the parents who raised us! But in these contemporary times, God intends to raise a new crop of parents. His intention is for the development channel of continuity in good parenting. The scripture makes it clear, with being born again, the old has gone and the new has come.

It is high time for our generation married, or unmarried, to stop thinking and complaining about what was and begin to think of what needs to be done right, by reflecting on where it all went wrong. If our parents had waited until they became parents before they knew how to parent, that would have had a negative effect on us. Therefore, we have to think of how to parent before becoming parents; setting standards and structures that we feel are needed to accomplish that vision beforehand.

The previous generation of parents trained and raised their children- that is us- the best way they could. Now is our turn to raise our God-given children better than we were raised. It will be for the good and well-being of our society and the world at large.

In the last book I wrote titled, *The Role of Parents in Childhood Development,* I was primarily concerned about the expectations children would often place on their parents, some met and some not. In this edition, I address a generation of parents that (i) are saddled with the responsibility of raising world changers and (ii) that would not just depend on their strength, ability, and knowledge to parent but would also be willing to unlearn and relearn better ways of parenting that is found in God alone.

As the enemy of man, the devil is devising new strategies to lure and seize children from being raised properly. God has already outlaid strategies from the beginning of the creation that best suit this era of parents. He intends to know and walk by these strategies, to breathe life again into a dying world, in order to bring glory and reverence to Him. Remember, it was Him who said, "let the little children come to me, and do not hinder them from me." And yet many children have been ignorantly denied access to God.

So, what's the way out? To keep complaining and pointing accusatory fingers while also believing that there is no hope to do something to restore them? Or begin to take responsibility, believing that if things have gone bizarre as a result of known and unknown factors, there would also be a set of people and parents who can rise and begin to change the course of time which will eventually birth a new day and pattern? It used to be the responsibility of our parents. Now it is ours. After all, they did their best. It is time for you and me to do better, to build upon what we have met and received.

This is a clarion call, and I hope that every youth, young couple, and even older parents will not just read, but take their place, where necessary, to call things to order by the grace of God. There is no impossibility with Him. Thus, if you have lost hope, I assure you there is still hope as long as you live. There is room to make amends.

In the course of writing this book, I've been exposed to better ways to raise my own children the right way.

This book is divided into four parts which focuses on: The Child's Development and Good Parenting, the Influence of the Generational Gap, Handling the Challenges of Adolescence and The Teacher, for Educational and Moral Child Upbringing.

These four parts center around the child and his need for becoming that better person his parents hope to see.

Hope comes to action when you notice that your strength is failing, and when your mind seems to be made up of not going beyond that point, there seems to be a need to revive and strengthen the last hope left in you– it is the light needed to push you to the end of the journey or the race. It is believed that where hope ceases to exist, life can be said to also not exist.

Most families are heartbroken because of issues experienced in recent times with children; some have lost their ways in the race, thereby causing grief to parents, who have almost lost out on options. Prayers seem to be mere words, advice seem to be mere words, and so on, so that at the mention of prayer, it seems as if it will not work.

But the scriptures make it clear that God is with us always; irrespective of the situation that besets you as a parent, God is still God and will do what seems best for him.

Going into some communities, you see a lot of negative activities going on that also make you wonder if there really is still hope that children and the family will become a happy place again. Children putting distance from parents and parents seem to be busy at their own end not noticing the fall out which could be catastrophic unless swift action is taken.

Whenever you see a light getting dim, you do not conclude that it is actually dead, because one fern on the dim light can spark it up again bringing about warmth to people. Another illustration is that of an athlete participating in a competition, and suddenly, he falls and all the spectators now look dismayed because they feel all hope of him winning the race is lost, but suddenly, he braces up again in whatever position he is and leaps, and that cheer begins to echo and he takes a step after another and on he goes until he finishes the race amongst the top three.

Such is the situation that surrounds us, and most especially the family. Some situations faced seem to give you a negative view of becoming a victor; but that one time you arise and become determined might be the spark needed to victory.

Reading this book should spark whatever hope that has been lost in you. It may be that the background you come from is faulty, but there is hope; it might be that you have been broken in that marriage, thereby causing you a lot of grief, and still, there is hope; it might be that your efforts as a child in the family are never noticed, there is still hope; and it might be that you have taken up a lonely part in life that seems to weigh you down to see to a new day in your family, there is still hope. Hope is a hidden price, just like the gold that if you don't understand its worth, you can neglect it and make it irrelevant, but the moment you do make it relevant, it becomes another priceless possession you will love to preserve.

So, are you a parent, couple, youth, or even a child? Preserve that hope in you until it gives you a reason to smile, and remember also, it might take long, but it won't be denied.

Table of Contents

PART ONE

Development And Good Parenting

Chapter 1

The Child

A poet, Stanley Chijioke Apugo, wrote a poem called, "Precious Little Ones"—

They are born and bred in our families,

They are innocent, with no limits to their rising,

They grow each day, watching all the happenings.

These little ones so bright will keep shining,

These precious ones are blessed with life so promising.

These are the next generation for whom we'll keep standing.

They come into our lives tender and cute.

They have so much to offer while they grow,

This we owe them; good nurture and care.

This they deserve; right training until they are old.

They are treasures from God whom we owe.

They are gifts from God who so cares.

These ones are so pure, gentle and lovely.

Angelic in looks, with radiant smiles.

They can make any man homely,

They can make any father run long miles.

This, they have turned us into.

This, they have made us into.

They are the future we look towards,

They are the jewels of the virtuous home.

We see them each day,

We need them each day,

I'm blessed to have them too,

For they always make my day.

Definition

Biologically, a child is a human between the stages of birth and puberty. In other words, a child generally refers to a minor, otherwise known as a person younger than the age of maturity.

A child can also be a person with a simple and soft heart who is ready to accept corrections and take words of advice which can be imparted in different ways: educationally, spiritually, physically, etc. for upbringing in a good manner that will help him/her in achieving greater heights in life.

Children are among the most sensitive and perceptive people you will ever find. Rebellion often comes during the time of teenage years when they feel their parents are asking them to behave in a way that is not consistent with what they like. It is very difficult to be citing examples of all the morals and values we hold dear, but that is one of the responsibilities we take on when we decide to be parents.

A child is also someone who has not reached adulthood; limited in size, physical assets, and mental reasoning. As a result of being a minor, the child is minor in reasoning and self-control in every sense. That is why handling criminal cases that pertain to children usually differs from that of adults. The offence might be committed out of ignorance of the law.

Of course, some of them may be wiser than their present age, say below 16 years of age. Such are exceptions and cannot be exempted from the category of minors in thinking and behaviour.

A child is thus an innocent, empty being, gifted to parents and the society. God expects parents to help them grow and develop a physical and spiritual impartation in their earthly journey.

Growth Stages Of A Child's Life

Every child goes through many stages of social development in life. At each of these stages, the child learns something that either benefits or endangers them. The child's life stages includes - infancy, toddler, preschool, primary school age, and adolescence. However, our basic concern will be on three of these stages.

Infancy/First stage

This is the first stage in a child's life. It is expected that, after nine months, the child should have developed in the womb which brings out the final result; a new born baby. After that, comes the naming ceremony of the child and dedication, which is normally done in a church or other places of worship and accompanied by a prayer and blessings for success and long life, hoping that the child will grow in the knowledge of God. It is expected that every child should be dedicated not only because the Bible said so, but also because that is another way of giving thanks to God.

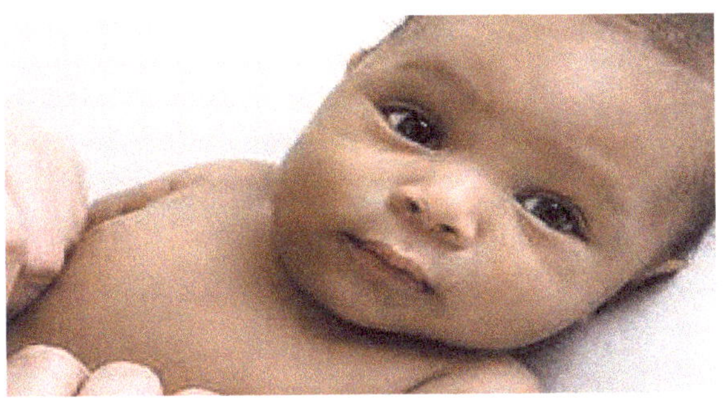

A baby/infant (Source: Picturesque)

The child is then sent to school to be educated and learn other aspects of life and training that he/she might and will not learn in the family. This stage often terminates at the age of twelve when going to secondary school or college.

The Adolescent Stage (Teenage):

It begins from the age of thirteen and is a crucial and sensitive stage in the child's life. At this point/stage, the child begins the second level of education which is either in a boarding or day setting/school. The child is then exposed to friends of different backgrounds. Making decisions and choices becomes an area of interest for the child at this stage because any choice/decision taken by them might benefit/endanger the child's life and future career/ambition. It might prove difficult at first but would later be easy as the child begins to learn to make the right choices in life. This can only be successful and effective when parents see it as their responsibility to stand in the place of prayer to support the child to make choices that will help him/her and that will not bring regret or shame to the family's reputation. Christ was twelve years of age when He knew the right thing/choice to take, "to be in my father's house" (Luke 2:49).

Young Adults (Source: Picturesque)

The Maturity Age

This starts from eighteen. In some western countries, at this age, most children go to colleges; some seek a job, pursuing their careers to have a sense of "independence" and a mandate to make decisions. However, in most African societies, at this stage, the individual is still under the control of his/her parents. They are, therefore, limited in making decisions at will because of the higher authority in the house. Parents need to realize that raising children of this age bracket is very challenging as it is now that they try to discover themselves as well as attempt to be independent, thus ignoring parental influence and restrictions.

Due to this factor, influences from parents make little or no impact while those of peer groups tend to fascinate them more. But it seems that reaching the age of twenty erupts into something else. God knows that something biological occurs at age twenty, which medical sources have recently discovered. When numbering the Hebrew men, God began at age twenty up to sixty, requiring half a shekel for redemption from that age, (Leviticus 27:3-5) All men over twenty were prepared for war if needed. Thus, God commanded Moses, "

Take a census of all the children of Israel by families, by their father's houses, according to the number of names, every name individually from twenty years old and above – all who are able to go to war in Israel. You and Aaron shall number them by their names" Numbers 1:2-3 (Stone, 2009).

This is to say that age twenty is significant in the life of every child, and parents need to be watchful as well at this stage.

Stone (2009) says, "What did God know about age twenty that we do not? In *For Parents Only*, the author reports why teenagers seeking their freedom often take foolish and dangerous decisions, ignoring obvious warnings. The author wrote: *"Our children/teens are not only addicted; they are also brain deficient. Science demonstrates that the frontal lobe of the brain – the area that allows judgement for consequences and control of impulses – does not fully develop until after the teen years. So, in the absence of a fully functioning frontal lobe, teenage brains rely more on the centres that control emotion – which in effect means they give in much easily to impulses.*

Society places heavy responsibilities on teenagers to make major decisions about career, college/institution and so on, at age eighteen, when in reality the teen mental judgement for such decision is better developed after the teen years. Obviously, the Creator knows that at age twenty and beyond, the judgement and reasoning frontal lobe of the brain was fully developed, allowing for better decision making and mental judgement… At age thirteen, children are affirmed into adulthood, but at age twenty, they become adults." (Perry Stone, 2009).

The Importance Of Childhood

When a parent loses out on child training at the early stage, it becomes difficult for them to make up for it in the future. Those early stages tend to be the appropriate time during which parents have to inculcate all the virtues that the child needs for their development. Those virtues would keep the child moving for the rest of his/her life, even when factors that would make them drift present themselves. Unfortunately, most parents prioritize pursuing a career– though not bad in itself – at the expense of having time to raise their children leaving them at the mercy of house-keepers, teachers, peers, neighbors and the society at large. The end result in most cases are bad influences on the child such as all manners of abuse; from sexual to verbal abuse and behavior that cause trauma that could stigmatize the child for a long time and sometimes for a life time.

Childhood is probably the most critical stage in the life of human beings. Therefore, it must be handled and treated with care and seriousness. Bishop Alexander drove this point home when he insisted that every aspect of the life of man, namely, their character, sense of responsibility, good and bad habits, ability to cope with difficulties, and piety are shaped primarily during childhood. (Alexander, ----).

What the child later remembers are those things which they cherished most recently in life. Those cherished moments become relevant and are considered the best moments of their lives. It follows therefore, that if a child grows up without parental care, the child will find it difficult to cope with the challenges of adulthood. Compare a child that grows up in an environment that exposes him/her to different choices, with one that struggles to make it in life. The latter might not cope, forcing them to either give up or strive harder, depending on their prevailing circumstances.

The imprint of early impressions is obvious. Such children may never have had proper upbringing, and experienced lack of parental care and affection, especially when they were left under the care of strangers. Furthermore, the absence of a strong Christian religious influence and upbringing in particular, would no doubt manifest in a person's character. Some kind of a fissure may be seen and perceived in their spiritual character. It has also been observed that children have extraordinary receptive religious impressions. For example, a child is instinctively drawn towards everything that opens up the beauty and meaning of life. If this is not introduced to them early in life or is taken away from them, their spiritual mind is likely to become weak or dampened, and may develop the feeling of loneliness, and eventually exhibit aggressive, unfriendly, and cruel tendencies against those they may meet later in life.

It has also been observed that even in physical development, children may be affected positively or negatively, depending on the nature of the environment they spend the better part of their childhood in. For example, a child who lived and grew up in an environment which was not friendly, had poor facilities, and crowded his physical, mental and emotional development may be negatively affected. The opposite is the case if the child finds spacious, well ventilated, and friendly habitation.

Most often, prominent and successful people, especially people who have impacted positively on their immediate or wider environments, and have displayed great integrity, energy and have lived purposeful lives must have come from backgrounds that were friendly, with hard-working families, or were brought up in environments with strong Christian religious backgrounds. Likewise, it is possible for prominent and successful people to have never had such backgrounds, but they always work extra-hard with much difficulty and pain, enduring the rough paths of life to be able to impact positively on their immediate or wider environments as well.

Later in life, even when such a person becomes weak in Christian faith, the experience he has acquired would play an important role in his restoration. The Lord will not abandon one who has carried the seed of goodness deep in his/her heart during childhood. It was not without foundation and justification when the writer of Proverbs said: **"Train a child in the way he should go, and when he is old he will not turn from it." (Prov. 22:6 –NIV)**

The word "mother" or "mothers" appears in the Bible almost 300 times. Since Biblical times, motherhood has been regarded as the highest honour that could be given to a married woman. Any woman who gave birth, especially to a male-child was the embodiment of a good woman leading a good marriage. And this is still true of certain cultures in our contemporary times.

Most godly pregnant-mothers would pray as they lay their hands on their stomach, sing praise and worship songs or recite the word of God to the unborn child. It is a means of guarding their soul and spirit, because the nine-months pregnancy phase is very critical to their well-being as well as the well-being of their unborn child. During this stage, when the child is most vulnerable the mother is careful to reside in an atmosphere of peace. She is aware that whatever happens to her affects the child in the womb. This practice is a process of spiritual impartation.

After the birth of the child, the mother influences its growth even more. She spends more time with her new-born, feeding, cleaning or changing diapers, cuddling and taking general care that is necessary for the baby's comfort. A good mother is selfless, putting the needs of her child above hers. This is her God-given design which includes taking the seed from the man, incubating it, and nourishing it afterrelease through childbirth.

Furthermore, a mother has a special type of influence on her child which is different from the influence of the father. From conception until the child leaves home, there is a unique bond that God has instilled in a mother–child relationship. Proverbs 1:8-9 says, "My son, hear the instruction of thy father, and forsake not the law of thy mother: For they shall be an ornament of grace unto thy head, and chains about thy neck."

Children are agents of change that God wants to use to make the world a better place. So whether you are a Christian, Muslim or a Traditional parent, God has given you children to raise them to become a medium of change for the world, for good. And I dare say, if our earthly parents will each take the responsibility of raising their children seriously, then the whole world will be occupied with good people working towards the good of humanity. It looks obvious that it is our negligence and ignorance that has led to the world's current depravity.

Responsibilities Of Parents Towards Their Children

Every parent has a vital role to play in his/her Child's development, physical, spiritual, educational, social, mental and so on. We are going to look at few basic aspects which include:

Provision: It is the duty of parents to provide the necessities of life to their children and the family, which include clothes, food, shelter, discipline, care, protection, love, and the best needed, as well as effective training for the child's development etc.

Discipline: The Bible tells us in Proverbs 13:24, **"he who spares the rod hates his son, but he who loves him is careful to discipline"** NIV. There is nothing good in ignoring a child when he/she does the wrong thing. Trying to please or not to offend the child can only spoil the child, but when you discipline the child, you not only correct that child but safeguard his/her future from damage as well. When you ignore your child's mistakes, you ruin the child's life, but when you correct his/her mistakes you keep the child from falling into a pit.

To teach: Joshua 1:8 tells us, "do not let this book of the law depart from your mouth; meditate on it day and night so that you may be careful to do everything written. Then you will be prosperous and successful" NIV. Also, Deuteronomy 6:6-9 says: "never forget this command that I am giving you today. Teach them to your children; repeat them when you are at home and when you are away; when you are resting and when you are working. Tie them on your arms and wear them on your forehead as a reminder. Write them on the doorpost of your houses and your gates". There are different ways to teach your child, and these include:

1. Rebuking: Proverbs 27:5 says, "better is open rebuke than hidden love" NIV.

2. Advising them on what to do to help build their future and avoiding paths in life that entangles/destroys.

3. Correcting the child helps him/her in life and leads to mutual understanding (i.e., the child knowing that the correction meted is for his/her good and benefit and the parent knowing that to ignore correcting the child becomes bad and sinful, because Proverbs 22:15 sums it all, "foolishness is bound in the heart of a child, but the rod of correction shall drive it far from him/her, KJV. However, all corrections should be administered in love.

4. Training in righteousness: Proverbs 22:6 says, "Train a child in the way he should go, and when he is old, he will not turn from it".

Mother and Child Discussing (Picturesque)

Looking at these ways of teaching, 2 Timothy 3:16 sums them all, "all scriptures is God – breathed and is useful for teaching, rebuking, correcting and training in righteousness. So the man (child) of God may be thoroughly equipped for every good work". So teaching the child helps him/her to be equipped in all manners of work in life as well as preparing for the sake of the future.

To be Responsible: It is also the parents' responsibility to teach them to be responsible in all aspects of life, as well as sending them to school to learn good morals. So, when they are educated, they help in contributing to the development of their society through all they have acquired, by being responsible citizens and good and effective leaders. Other ways of teaching a child to be responsible include being kind, patient, being hopeful, disciplined, giving simple chores, talking about God, engaging in meaningful activities and speaking helpful things that will build the children and not destroy them.

To Love and pay attention to them: This is a worrisome issue in our society today. Children deviate easily from the right path to the wrong path without the notice of parents, because of their schedules/activities that makes it difficult to give quality time and attention to the child's development. When you spend time with your child, it helps the child to trust you and be able to share issues that bothers him/her with you, and seek advice on what to do and solutions on how to go about solving the problem. Lack of these tend to be some of the reasons why our society gets worse in some areas, because when a child loses the love and attention of parents, he/she gets involved with bad companies/friends with the aim of getting that love and attention missing/lost in the home.

Parents, the future of your children can only be tampered with if you let them go their way, which always ends in regret and worry for some parents. But when you give them that attention, love and care as well as your time, they will not go outside or mingle or meet friends that will lead them astray, but will always run to you, as well as love to walk with friends that they know they will build each other's future and not ruin it.

Teach them to pray: It is believed that in most Christian families, before a child is born, most parents always pray for the unborn baby by placing their hands on the mother's belly.

A Child who has been taught to pray

Teaching a child how to pray in the womb is a vital way of introducing him/her to Jesus and reinforcing their relationship with God. Our Lord gave us prayer so we could communicate with Him directly. So making children familiar with prayer helps them to understand that God is always close and accessible to them at any time and place, so they can call upon Him not only in trouble but at all times. A child can be taught how to pray by starting from simple words as it gradually improves. No child who learns how to pray from childhood will tell you he/she never appreciates it, so the best time to help your child know how to pray is when he/she is still young, so that he/she can make it a habit later in life.

"The efforts which a mother makes for the improvement of her child in knowledge and virtue, are necessarily retired and unobtrusive. The world knows nothing of them; and hence the world has been slow to perceive how powerful and extensive is this secret and silent influence….the influence which is exerted upon the mind during the first eight or ten years of existence, in a great degree guides the destinies of that mind for time and eternity! And as the mother is the guardian and guide of the early years of life, from her goes the most powerful influence in the formation of the character of man." John Abbott

When parents stop being "Kingdom-minded", they stop making Kingdom choices. Choices like devoting a life to raising the next generation to love God, to honour authority and to live wisely. The very church of Christ has so degraded the blessing of children, that it is almost unthinkably ignorant. For how can we expect to pass the torch of passion and faithfulness of our Saviour unless we have made it our sole aim, to daily impress His character into the hearts of our children?

When we understand that our whole existence is to glorify the Lord, we live each moment differently. *We get about our Father's business.* We don't measure "if we should have children" by their convenience or how many vacations it will cost us or whether we can pursue my favourite pastime or career. We don't have children to make them look cute in their ball uniforms and homemade hair bows.

We fall down on our knees with the grave responsibility of stewardship over these children, these people who will either further the Kingdom or be a blight on society, based largely on our diligence to the duty of raising them.

Parents, you must govern your home well. It is the cruelest act of parenthood to neglect teaching your children to obey the loving authority over them. For in doing so, you make them unable to submit to God.

Children who have not learned self-government stand to be the most wretched of all men and women, loathing you for your indulgences.

But don't you see, it is not harsh! It wells up from the deepest love, the deepest desire to see our children walking in truth, and evokes sheer delight to walk beside them.

When you see your children through Kingdom-eyes, their voices are not irritations that bug you and cause you to be angry; they are offences that sober you and call you to the tireless and tender action of praying for, teaching and tending the garden of their souls, which is also in a constant battle of what is arising from within them.

Your children will be the happiest when you love them enough to require gratitude, obedience and honour. Their little faces light up into yours when they sense your utmost sincerity towards their character.

"Ponder all the life-implications of a well-controlled adult and see if he will not look back on his devoted mother with all the gratitude his life can muster and attribute to her the bulk of his earthly successes!"

This "imparting of wisdom" is not just a nice parenting term to toss around; it plays itself out day by day, hour by hour, in the details of life. Someone is there beside our children every day, pointing them to wisdom or foolishness, teaching them in all things, whether right or wrong.

Anyone who has been home all day with little ones knows the enormous time and mental energy it takes to raise children.

Children According to Jesus: If You Want to See the Kingdom

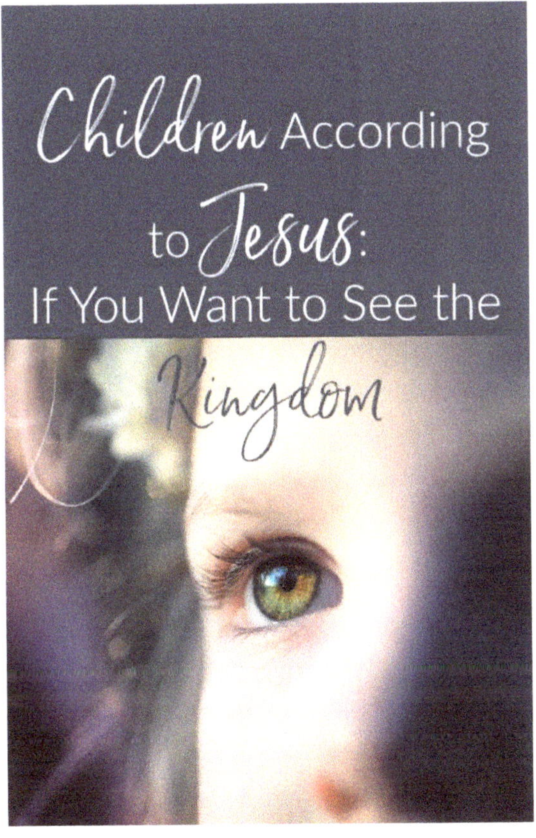

We view children backwards. Jesus' disciples did too

"Jesus, tell them to take their children away–they're interfering." (paraphrased, of course).

Jesus said, "Do not forbid the children to come unto me for of such is the Kingdom of Heaven."

And in other places He said, "Unless you humble yourselves and become as one of these little children, you will not see the Kingdom of God."

And of course, "Children are a heritage from the Lord, a gift and a blessing, Blessed is the man whose quiver is full."

We mostly make decisions about whether to have a child, or how many to have based on what we want. Will it change our standard of living? What will be best for our reputation? How easy will it be to vacation? Will I get more stretch marks? Can we afford daycare? Will I have to quit my job? Almost always, we think of children as another liability to our lives. Or, occasionally as an asset: whether we can make them into something successful–our trophies, if you will. Either way, we usually look at them in terms of how they will change our lives outwardly.

The **children God gives you have so much more to do with revealing Himself to you and making you more fit for His purposes.** It's really not about how cute they look dressed up in white linen, or whether they grow up to play Beethoven well. Those things are wonderful– perks even, but I believe children are really given to us to change us and make us more like the Giver Himself.

Things God can and is teaching parents through the children he gave them;

- Forgive quickly–never hold grudges.
- There is a lot to smile about.
- Don't let the cares of the world dampen the miraculous thrill of creation– a newly discovered caterpillar is worth careful observation.

- We don't have to be taught how to sin.
- We have to practice good habits or the bad ones take over naturally.
- Stronger faith.
- Patience—ever so slowly.
- Sometimes crying just makes it better.
- There is no such thing as too many hugs.
- God's creativity is mind-blowing.
- Honesty should be tamed before it leaves the mouth.
- No matter how many times I mess up, my Father still loves me.
- A regular routine is a very healthy thing.
- Home is a good place to be.
- Working is the best recipe for peace and contentment.
- You can't have too many Legos.
- The fewer trips we can make to Wal-Mart, the better.
- Skin colour doesn't make a difference.
- Name brands or brand of car doesn't either.
- Joyfulness doesn't depend on my circumstances.
- Heaven is real and we should be excited about going there.
- Couch cushions on the floor are just as good as amusement parks.
- You miss a lot when you're in a hurry.
- Christmas just keeps getting more fun.
- Every single child is completely unique, a fresh thought of God, and brings a joy to my life I would have otherwise missed.
- The most important things on earth are the people in your life— and the older you get, the more important they become.

Chapter 2

Characteristics of Child Developmental Stages

Below are some of the most visible characteristics of children and youth. The period taken into consideration falls between the ages of one to sixteen.

1 – 4 years old

General Characteristics

1. They are unique children, with their own rhythms and strategies.
2. They build on their reflexes and sensory-motor experience to develop as a person.
3. They are socially dependent, developing trust.
4. They respond interactively to faces, talking, cooing.
5. They reach out searching for a response, and evoking responses in others.
6. Always falling in love with particular adults.
7. Sometimes withdraw into sleep from over stimulation; or may express their unhappiness or grief by crying.

Physical Characteristics

1. Attention, social contact with adults who see them different from others.
2. Sense of well-being.
3. Love a variety of colours, textures and sounds which stimulates their exploration.
4. Warm quick response: physical and eye contact.

5. Prone to touch and be touched; safety, secure space to move, master new body skills.

6. Are moved to and stimulated by interesting things and happenings.

7. Interested in people who grant them access to do what pleases them.

8. Observe and touch objects, some that respond to their action on them.

Social Characteristics

1. Interested in children of the same age.

2. Are curious.

3. Always energetic.

4. Recognize parents and special people; and attach to special toys and things that can be seen and touched.

5. Dependent on particular adults.

6. Always playful.

7. Not yet enough control for toilet training.

8. Cooperative; working on conflict resolution problems.

Emotional Characteristics

1. They express their feelings through crying, facial expressions, and body language.

 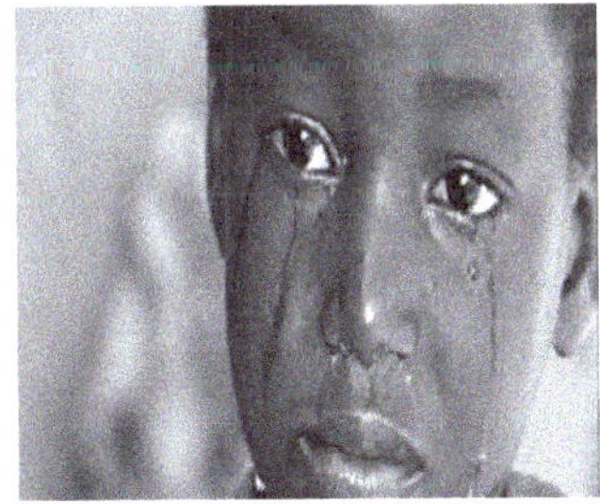

Child Emotions

2. Need trust and security.
3. They sometimes find it difficult to control their emotions.
4. They love expressing themselves, but need to be asked directly.

Mental Characteristics

1. Understand words and communicate through sounds and gestures.
2. Begin to develop language.
3. Judge based on understanding rather than logic.
4. Use symbols expertly at a specific level.
5. They need people who can read their behaviour and understand their language.

5 – 7 years' old

General Characteristics

1. Same sex activities and involment in opportunities of engaging in activities with their peer.
2. Interact with adults who take them seriously.
3. Involved in a lot of physical activities, sports, dancing, etc.
4. Connected to groups that share their interests and talents, even adult groups.

Physical Characteristics

1. Very active.
2. Are verbal.
3. Enjoy a sense of humour.
4. Acquire skills both physical as well as reading and numbers.
5. Becoming socially competent.

6. Peers are very important to them at this stage.
7. Increasingly independent and self-sufficient.
8. Excited when helping in the family, school or environment e.t.c

Social Characteristics

1. Team and group support and need peer group recognition.
2. Unique in certain areas, often talented and need special encouragement.
3. Are physically active.
4. Girls and boys become more separate, recognize and express negative feelings toward the other gender.

Mental Characteristics

1. They need to be constantly reminded so as not to forget easily.
2. Need encouragement and not just praise for their work and play.
3. Enjoy group activities, and things that have less value such as sports etc.
4. Prefer to be monitored when doing something productive to keep them safe and assured of safety.
5. They learn best by being involved.
6. They are very imaginative and eager to know about things.

Emotional Characteristics

1. Express their feelings when hurt.
2. Expect respect and motivation from adults.
3. Establish their feelings on a particular thing.
4. They can become frustrated when things don't turn out as expected.
5. Interested in the feelings of their family, community, and culture.

8 – 10 Years Old

General characteristics

1. Interested in people: aware of differences, willing to give more to others, but also expecting a lot from others.
2. Busy, active, full of enthusiasm, may try too much to be pleasers than offenders, interested in money and its value.
3. Sensitive to criticism, recognize failure, capacity for self-evaluation.
4. Capable of prolonged interest.
5. Decisive, dependable, reasonable, strong sense of right and wrong.
6. Spend a great deal of time in discussion. Often outspoken and critical of adults, although still dependent on approval.

Physical characteristics

1. Very active: need frequent breaks from tasks to have fun and energetic things.
2. Bone growth is not yet complete.
3. Some may mature early, may be insecure about their appearance or size.
4. Often accident prone.

Social characteristics

1. Start to develop close ties with friends outside the family and start to seek independence.
2. Very choosy about friends, acceptance by them is important.
3. Can be competitive.
4. Team games become popular.
5. May try to emulate popular sports heroes and TV and movie stars.

Emotional characteristics

1. Very sensitive to praise and recognition; feelings are hurt easily.
2. Because friends are so important during this time, there can be conflicts between adult rules and friends' influence. Mentors can help with honesty and consistency.

Mental characteristics

1. Fairness is very important to them.
2. Eager to answer questions and look for a positive response to their ideas.
3. Very curious; like to collect things but may jump to other objects of interest after a short time.
4. Want more independence but look for guidance and support.
5. Reading abilities vary widely.

Developmental tasks

1. Social cooperation.
2. Self-evaluation.
3. Skill learning.
4. Team play.

Suggested volunteer strategies

1. Recognize allegiance to friends and heroes.
2. Help them understand responsibilities in a two-way relationship.
3. Acknowledge and praise performance and support them often.
4. Offer enjoyable learning experience; share ideas about different cultures and fun facts about geography to broaden their sense of the world around them.
5. Provide frank answers to questions.

Suggested activities

1. Introduce new games that will broaden their concepts of different cultures.
2. Video games.
3. Board games.
4. Craft projects and drawing; remember to display their work.
5. Get to know who and what they are interested in and who they are trying to emulate in pop culture.
6. Engage in educational games that allow them to see the fun in learning.

11 – 13 Years Old

General characteristics

1. Testing limits, "know-it-all" attitude.
2. Identify with an admired adult; may reflect examples of that adult.
3. Vulnerable, emotionally insecure, fear of rejection and mood swings.
4. Bodies are going through physical changes that affect personal appearance.

Physical characteristics

1. Small-muscle coordination is good.
2. Bone growth is not yet complete.
3. Are very concerned with their appearance and very self-conscious about growth.
4. Diet and sleep habits can be bad or inconsistent, which may result in low energy levels.
5. Girls may begin menstruation.

Social characteristics

1. Acceptance by friends becomes quite important.
2. Cliques start to develop.
3. Team games are popular.
4. Crushes on members of the opposite sex are common.
5. Friends set the general rule of behaviour.
6. Feel a real need to conform; may dress and behave alike in order to belong.
7. Very concerned about what others say and think of them.
8. Have a tendency to manipulate others.
9. Interested in earning their own money.
10. Start to develop ideas of their future.

Emotional characteristics

1. Very sensitive to praise and recognition; feelings are hurt easily.
2. Can be hard to balance adults' rules and friend's rules.
3. Are caught between being a child and being an adult.
4. Need praise as an individual to distinguish themselves from the group.
5. Loud behaviour hides a lack of self-confidence.
6. Look at the world more objectively, at adults subjectively and critically.

Mental Characteristics

1. Perfectionists. Don't know their own limitations; may try to do too much and may feel frustrated and guilty.
2. Want more independence, but often still need guidance and support, which they might reject.
3. Attention span can be lengthy.
4. Are exploring boundaries and discovering consequences of behaviour.
5. May seek guidance and advice from a trusted friend.

Developmental Tasks

1. Social cooperation.
2. Self-evaluation.
3. Skill learning.
4. Team play.

Suggested Volunteer Strategies

1. Offer alternative opinions without being insistent.
2. Accepting different physical states and emotional changes in their lives.
3. Give frank answers to questions.
4. Share aspects of professional life and rewards of achievement in work.
5. Do not tease about appearance, clothes, boy/girlfriends, or sexuality. Affirm often.

Suggested Activities

1. Trivial Pursuit.
2. Help with homework.
3. Creative writing; this can get them to express their thoughts and ideas in a very beneficial and positive way.
4. Watch educational videos about the changes they might experience in adolescence.
5. Have discussions with them, and actually listen, letting them know that how they feel is important.
6. Read plays with them; broaden their horizons while letting them know that learning can be fun.

14 –16 Years Old

General Characteristics

1. Testing limits, "know-it-all" attitude.
2. Face challenges of developing mentally and physically.

3. Vulnerable, emotionally insecure, fear of rejection, mood swings.
4. Often project competence while lacking full ability.
5. Identify with an admired adult, or often reject adults in exchange for friends.

Physical Characteristics

1. Very concerned and self-conscious with their appearance and growth.
2. Diet and sleep habits can be uneven, which may result in low energy levels.
3. May experience rapid weight gain at the beginning of adolescence. Enormous appetite.
4. Desire to learn good personal hygiene and grooming.

Social Characteristics

1. Friends set the general rules of behaviour.
2. Feel a real need to conform. They dress and behave alike in order to "belong"
3. Are very concerned about what others say and think of them.
4. Go to extremes; emotional instability with a "know-it-all" attitude.
5. Fear of ridicule and of being unpopular.
6. Often facing duality of childhood and adulthood in adolescence.
7. Girls are usually more interested in boys than vice versa, because of early maturity.

Emotional Characteristics

1. Are very sensitive to praise and recognition; feelings are easily hurt.
2. Are caught between being a child and being an adult.
3. Self-confidence is a very important factor in going against peer pressure and concern for success.

4. Loud behaviour hides their lack of self-confidence.

5. Look at the world more objectively, but look at adults subjectively, and may be critical.

Mental Characteristics

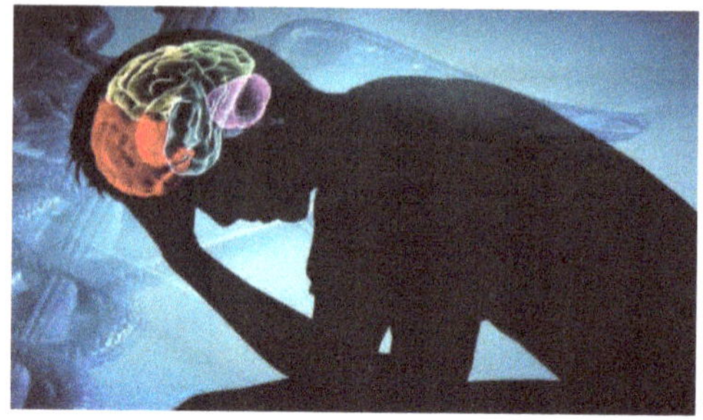

Image, showing the mental structure of a teen

(Source: Picturesque)

1. Can better understand moral principles.

2. Thought processes are starting to involve more of their own personal voice.

3. Attention span can be lengthy.

4. Argumentative behaviour may be part of "trying out" an opinion.

Developmental Tasks

1. Physical maturation.

2. Abstract thinking.

3. Strong sense of responsibility and consequences.

4. Membership in a peer group is important.

5. Developing more defined relationships among their peers.

Suggested Volunteer Strategies

1. Give choices and don't be afraid to confront inappropriate behaviour.
2. Use humour to diffuse tense situations.
3. Give positive feedback, and let the mentee know affection is for them and not for accomplishments.
4. Be available and be yourself with strengths, weaknesses and emotions.
5. Be honest and disclose appropriate personal information to build trust.
6. Apologize when appropriate.

Suggested Activities

1. Shared community service projects such as volunteering to do a canned food drive before the holidays.
2. Help with homework, while stressing the importance of homework as a priority.
3. Creative writing and development of poetry.
4. Discussion: tap into how they view things and let them know that their points of view are important.

Chapter 3

Notable Children with Remarkable Parental Impact

Firstly, let me remind you that parents are supposed to be role models to their children. The way you model your child is how they will turn out to be; the child's first model is his/her parents.

Dear Parents, you have major roles to play because the children come into the world through you. They grow with you until they are mature enough to live independent of you. You will probably transit to glory before them. It implies that most of their early life, when they are vulnerable, is spent with you.

Other people and institutions of the society, such as school and church, also play several roles to further develop the child. While the church grooms the children spiritually, the school grooms them educationally, mentally and socially.

In fact, the school is the second key institution in raising the child, because teachers spend between 8 and 30 hours every week with the child, depending on their age and learning status. They serve as a vital intermediary, in terms of learning, between the home and society for the child.

It is general knowledge that what you give your time to, would be shaped/moulded according to the pattern or taste you may have envisioned for it to become. In this chapter we will be looking at examples of parents who influenced their children such that they became agents of positive change benefiting the whole world today.

Esther –Mordecai (Esther Chapters 1-10)

Esther was an obedient Jewish girl at a young age, but because of captivity found herself in Susa. She had learnt the Jewish tradition and culture from her uncle Mordecai so well that she would not readily disclose her identity (Esther2:10).

When there was the need for a new Queen of Persia, Esther was among the ladies selected to be trained for six months by the chief Eunuch, before their presentation to the King for the choosing of a Queen (Esther 2:12-14).

What the Kingdom was looking out for in the young maidens was beyond the standards of beauty and family background. A woman with a noble character who would be an example to other women was their target. Esther won the contest. I then ask if the parents of the other maidens did not do well in raising their daughters? Or was it because God had ordained it to be so? We should not forget that the Eunuch was there, who was the instructor of the maidens. To our youths, when in a new environment, learn to treat everyone with respect. In general, the person you disregard might just be the key to the inner room.

Since Mordecai might have taught Esther to show reverence to everyone, it included the Eunuch, who was always with the King. That was her access point, even though she never saw herself as the Queen yet. She only showed respect to everyone within the palace as part of her character, without any motive. And so, she was finally ushered to the King's presence at her appointed time.

The Bible shows Mordecai fulfilling the role of a diligent father to his young cousin, Esther, who had lost both parents (verse 7). Mordecai had instilled great wisdom, tact, humility and grace in her character. He commands respect and obedience from her (verse 20)—even after she becomes the queen!

Parents must teach their children boldness with respect, and not arrogance. While some lessons are taught, others are best obtained by observation of the learner. Perhaps, the key to the king's heart and throne was the Eunuch. Only Esther could discern this so she ascended the throne of a foreign land - Esther 2:17-18. "Xerxes liked Esther more than he did any of the other young women. None of them pleased him as much as she did, and he immediately fell in love with her and crowned her queen in place of Vashti" (V.17).

During the period of training, for her presentation as a candidate to be Ahasuerus' queen, Mordecai warns Esther to use her wisdom and not reveal that she was a Jew. He was being separated from the daughter that he had lovingly raised. But as a dutiful and loving father, he checked on her welfare daily (verse 11). Even after she was chosen, Mordecai stayed close to make sure she was alright, revealing himself as her father.

God has never denied parents the privilege of raising their children to take over territories, both physical and spiritual. Rather, the responsibility to see that it comes to pass lies solely with the parents. Mordecai understood that if Esther was trained well, she would not only cause change in the Palace and Susa alone but also to the whole Jewish race. And that was made manifest when Haman plotted against the Jews; Mordecai reminded her of where she was from and the reason why she was there at such a time. Once properly encouraged, Esther saw her responsibility before God and moved to accomplish it with humility, courage, and wisdom. At this point, the situation completely entrusted to God, He too moves to resolve the situation swiftly and equitably.

Parents, note that the day your children forget their identity or foundation, they lose an integral part of who they are. The child needs to consistently be reminded, so that when the day of liberation comes, they will stand with their people rather than the enemy (Esther 7:1-4).

When Esther found out that she was destined to be queen, she surrounded herself with faithful Jewish servants who provided her with kosher food and did not betray the fact that she was Jewish for Mordecai had told her to keep her ancestry a secret until the appropriate time for her to reveal her secret.

Mordecai was a human being just like us. He had someone entrusted to his care just as our children are given to us. He had a normal, mundane job that he apparently held diligently. When a critical situation arose, he took action, doing more than he had to. He never complained about not being immediately compensated. Even after doing everything to the best of his ability and trusting God, he sustained tremendous persecution, but his mind and heart never wavered. He patiently waited on God and his purpose.

Joseph and Jacob (Genesis 37)

Joseph was an outstanding personality, possibly because his father, Jacob, responded by showing him love to a default in return of his honest reportage of the mischievous activities of his older brothers. Every parent will always appreciate a child that is faithful and trustworthy.

Children must however learn to do what is expected of them so as to gain trust, reward and blessings from their parents. It therefore calls on the child to do what will make him or her earn the respect of his parents to avoid the thought of being envious of his/her other siblings.

At that moment, you have broken their hearts. Their reaction must show. But know that they still love you and are waiting expectantly for a change. Just like the prodigal son, because it is no parent's wish to treat his/her child differently from another, but when compelled, they will have to.

Joseph's life is a series of highs and lows — both literally and figuratively. In his father's house, Joseph was the favoured son. "Israel loved Joseph more than all his sons since he was a child of his old age" (Genesis 37:3). To demonstrate this preference, Jacob gifted Joseph with the famous *kitonet passim,* translated as a garment with long sleeves or a fine woollen tunic. This preferential treatment from their father elicited much jealousy from Joseph's ten older brothers.

Jacob was incidentally teaching Joseph (i) to know and serve the God of their forefathers diligently (ii) to be a faithful steward in all that his hands find doing and (iii) to be a good leader-what took place later in a foreign land.

God expects parents to stand at the epicentre of his grand plan and purpose - to raise children as models. Most times, they might not even comprehend it from the onset. But if they remain obedient and diligent, it will keep unfolding until the child fits into the plan orchestrated for them.

As a teenager, Joseph reports back to his father his older brothers' activities while tending to the flocks (Genesis 37:2). Joseph also shares his two dreams with the family. The first one in which his brothers' eleven sheaves of wheat bowed down to him, and the second, where the sun, moon, and eleven stars all bow to him. In each case, both his siblings and his parents interpreted the dreams as meaning that one day Joseph would rule over his family (Genesis 37:5-11). In fact, they got angry at the innocent dreamer.

Eventually the brothers acted on their emotions. Seeing the "dreamer" approach on a shepherding trip, they ambushed Joseph and threw him into a pit — the first of the great depths to which Joseph will sink. The brothers soon sold him to Midianite or Ishmaelite traders heading down to Egypt, continuing Joseph's descent. The brothers then tore up his special coat, dipped it in goat's blood, and presented it to Jacob, their father, as 'proof' of his son's death.

Joseph's time in Egypt is even more tumultuous than his life in Canaan. The Ishmaelite traders sold him as a slave to Potiphar- the captain of the Palace guard. Joseph finds great fortune with Potiphar, but his promotion in Potiphar's household attracts the attention of Potiphar's wife, who repeatedly seduces him. When her attempts fail, she accuses Joseph of rape, which lands him in prison, without fair hearing.

Though now in the deepest of his life's trenches, God is still with Joseph (Genesis 39:21). His fellow inmates, Pharaoh's former butler and baker, both dreamt symbolic dreams. Joseph interpreted that the butler will be exonerated in three days and restored to Pharaoh's service, and the baker will be put to death. And his interpretations came true.

Joseph asked the butler to remember him once he's back in Pharaoh's service, but the butler forgot until, two full years later, Pharaoh himself had disturbing dreams. These dreams turned out to be divine arrangements for Joseph to appear before Pharaoh. He is brought to the court to interpret two famous dreams of Pharaoh: one in which seven sickly cows consumed seven healthy cows, and a parallel dream in which seven sickly ears of grain consumed seven lush ears of grain.

Joseph tells Pharaoh: "Seven years are coming, a great abundance through the land. Then seven years of famine will arise" (Genesis 41:25-30). With this knowledge in hand, Pharaoh prepared Egypt for famine. Joseph, at the age of 30, is appointed second-in-command to Pharaoh.

It is worthy to note that Joseph's mother was the beloved wife of his father. While Jacob may be criticized for the kind of parenting he did, God in His sovereign plan knew what was going to happen, and provided the environment to make His plans for Joseph to unveil. Jacob, his entire family and the nation of Israel was thus God's grand design.

Solomon and David (1 Kings 1)

1 Chronicles 29:22-30

They made Solomon the son of David king (ver. 22). "Then Solomon sat on the throne... instead of David his father" (ver. 23). "And David died in a good old age. and Solomon his son re-joined in his stead" (ver. 28). We have our thoughts directed to the respective virtues of the two kings; father and son, and the comparative value of their life and reign. In some respects, they are open to comparison, but in others to contrast.

Both were

(1) kings of united Israel;
(2) servants of Jehovah;
(3) writers of inspired and immortal literature.

In the past, it was possible to find parents who stood upright with God and were able to raise a generation after them, who learnt equally from the same stream; but in our present day and time, it seems to be the other way round. Finding parents standing and the children they bear living contrary.

God told David his hands are full of blood so he cannot build a temple for Him, but his son whom he has chosen will build it on his behalf. Let me say, David shows examples of both a good and bad kind of parent, of all his children mentioned, before Solomon – Absalom (2 Samuel 13-18) and Adonijah (1 Kings 1:1-27) and Ammon (2 Samuel 13) shows an error. Absalom was a cunning child who needed the throne of his father and Israel at all cost, even to the point of trying to kill his father, and sleeping with his father's concubines; then I ask the question: who was giving him such counsel? Where was the mother who was to join hands with the father in raising that child? If really the mother was an Israelite, she should have known the law and rebuked her son, we all know his end; Adonijah who thought and knew that the throne rightly belongs to him but handed it to his brother, later lost both the throne and his life. All those thoughts birthed by these sons of David rose from a place that is not godly, because they all died miserably. David might have noticed the rising of the thought but ignored its development until it became a thorn in his neck, but he always repented and never permitted such a thing to happen again. And those were the things he used in building Solomon to become a better King. Every parent must always carry the thought of raising his/her children to become better than they are. So, if your spiritual level as a parent stops at you just reading the Bible and praying, you must pray, hope, expect and permit for the day that your child will read the Bible and Interpret it through the mind of the Spirit, praying with understanding, and learning discernment; and if you have, then you need to teach your son intimacy with the Holy Spirit so as not to be tossed by the wind of their day.

Solomon was born in <u>Jerusalem</u>, the second born child of <u>David</u> and his wife <u>Bathsheba</u>, widow of <u>Uriah the Hittite</u>. The first child, a son conceived of adultery during Uriah's lifetime, had died as a punishment on account of the death of Uriah by David's order. Solomon had three brothers born to Bathsheba named: <u>Nathan</u>, Shammua, and Shobab, besides six known older half-brothers born of as many mothers.

The biblical narrative shows that Solomon served as a peace offering between God and David, due to his adulterous relationship with Bathsheba. In an effort to hide this sin, for example, he sent the woman's husband to battle, hoping that he would be killed there. After he died, David was finally able to marry his wife. As punishment, the first child, who was conceived during the adulterous relationship, died. Solomon was born after David was forgiven. It is this reason why his name, which means peace, was chosen. Some historians cited that <u>Nathan the Prophet</u> brought up Solomon while his father was busy governing the realm. This could also be attributed to the notion that the prophet held great influence over David because he knew of his adultery, which was considered a grievous offense under the <u>Mosaic Law</u>. It was only during <u>Absalom</u>'s rebellion that Solomon started spending more time at David's side.

David realized this, so he had to take his time to teach and imbibe the right leadership skills Solomon needed when he ascended the throne. That's why when God asked Solomon what he needed, he opted for wisdom and understanding to lead the people of God, against any other thing (1 Kings 3), because wisdom is profitable to lead and direct. As a result of that, he not only was wise, but equally rich and the greatest that ever lived who spoke more words of wisdom than any other in the Scriptures; all this would not have come from any other place than from sitting at the feet of his father David.

Before his <u>death</u>, David gave his final admonition to his son, Solomon, saying, "Keep the charge of the Lord your God: to walk in his ways, to keep his statutes, his commandments, his judgments, and his testimonies, as it is written in the **Law** of **Moses**, that you may prosper in all that you do and wherever you turn for you are a wise man" (1 Kings 2).

So, when parents teach their children to learn and know the secrets in the Bible or word of God, it becomes the greatest asset they can use to ascend greater heights and levels of thought they never imagined. So as a parent, what asset are you passing unto your child/children?

Isaac and Abraham

The best gift parents can give and pass to their children is that of raising them to know, believe and hope in God for themselves; and entrusting them with the responsibility of raising godly children as they were raised to enhance continuity in the family line.

God's promise to Abraham was to make him father of all nations, but He never told him how that will come to pass. God gave him Isaac as the promised child and then demanded for the same promised child. Like I mentioned earlier, there are aspects of training that the child sees and learn, some they have to be thought; so that even when his father said "God will provide" the sacrificial lamb, first he trusted his father's words and I believe that is not the first time he saw and was informed by his father of how he trusted God who always supplied to them, and at the same time have heard the story surrounding his birth. Parents must teach, tell and must become examples to their children, because they are all children of promise as the parents are the carriers of the promised generation in God.

Isaac grew knowing the ways and God of his father, so that it was recorded "God of Abraham but dread of Isaac" – Genesis 31:42. He was taught and he learned until he went a step further to his father's walk with God. What an honour for Abraham to see his son walking in that pattern; I believe in God's plan for parenting children, it was never meant to be difficult, but because some parents could not see, understand and comprehend as well perceive the prophecy and plans of God over that child/children, it now makes it difficult for parents to parent.

Let me mention here that any parenting without discipline is not parenting; because in trying to work in the master plan of God, for making the children become what God wants them to be, does not mean he or she should not be disciplined. So the scripture emphasized "God opposes the proud, but gives grace to the humble"; because any child who is chastised or disciplined is humble and eats of the fruit, and any child who is not disciplined or chastised is arrogant and proud; so in that aspect of discipline, God is the unseen and unspoken aspect of training you don't know and can never imagine (except you have a good relationship with him). The child in its entirety is equally a spirit in a fleshly body, and as spirit, they respond to whatever their environment brings their way; so if the environment tends to be loose, they become loose too; if it is tight and strict, they adapt to it. As parents, you should not have a soft heart. When it comes to raising them in God's pattern, they might perceive and think in a negative manner in the first instance, but it's just for a time and they will learn to appreciate it.

If Abraham had wasted the God-given resources of God around him, Isaac would have done the same; but as he tendered and managed with all sense of faithfulness, Isaac learned how to equally manage the resources also. Parenting is sweet, but equally difficult if not understood properly. It goes beyond just giving birth, it goes into knowing that you are raising a generation of change makers and transformers. So when you raise your children well/ as it should be, be it in death or when still alive, you will be at peace, but when you don't you will always regret why you did not do it right. When it seems difficult, just know that with man it is not possible, but with God it is possible.

Josiah – Jedidiah (2 Kings 22-23)

Mothers must realize that they are not just "mothers" but influencers for great men and women who are to come from their womb. So if a mother has a positive influence over her child, it is revealed in the manner and behaviour of that child, and if it is negative, that also reveals over time.

Though Josiah was a promised child according to I Kings 13:2, one who will cleanse Israel in his day, but it had to be through a mother who will be able to risk whatever it takes to ensure that such prophecy comes to pass. Parents must never take prophecy for granted, most especially during dedication they must learn to believe and equally seek God's leadership on how they will work to see it come to pass. Josiah's father, Amon has not lived a life that pleased God but he had a wife who believed in God in the midst of the disbelieving system and was willing to go against all odds. She respects her King and husband to see that their child was raised to know and please the God of his fathers.

The major developmental stages of children are being done or carried most especially by mothers, and there is no limit to this stage. Josiah's mother knew that, and worked on that for the good of her son which made it easier to break out of the traditional culture and behaviour his fathers lived with, which was contrary to the pattern his ancestors and forefather had placed and followed from the beginning, altering the pattern of idol worship to the actual worship of the true God.

And that singular act recorded in the Bible was carried out by the young King Josiah at age 8, through the influence and upbringing of his mother. Which implies that a mother can have an ungodly man as husband but can still raise children according to the standard and plan God had designed for their child/children from the beginning; all that is expected of her in such cases is to believe and insist on her belief in those promises and not compromising until it is birthed and realized in the life of her children.

In the story of the virtuous woman in Proverbs 30, the scripture never mentioned that she did not know what to do when faced with troubles, she had the wisdom to discern, which gave her husband the edge and respect amongst his peers or fellow men. So mothers can be with an ungodly father as husband and still raise his integrity as well as teach other women how to raise their children as she is doing; who knows perhaps through that her husband will come to know God and forfeit those ungodly patterns or ways? You must know as a mother/parent, if another parent did it in a godly pattern and it was successful, you have equally been given the same mandate and privilege to work it out and make your dying family come alive again. This is to stress the fact that if Josiah's mother could raise her son to a position of prominence under a father who did not believe in God, you also can. For 8 years she was teaching and insisting on the culture and tradition of the patriarchs which had been set before them, and perhaps to the King who failed to listen to her. All God needs in such times, is one out of the two who believes and is willing to partner with him to make what is in his heart, pertaining that child, find expression.

Samuel – Hannah (1 Samuel)

Hannah was the preferred wife of Elkanah; a Levite from Ramah in Ephraim. Elkanah was also married to Peninnah. Now, the bible said that Peninnah had children; both daughters and sons but Hannah was childless, because the Lord had shut up her womb. Every year, Elkanah went out of the city to worship and make sacrifices to the Lord in Shiloh, which was the capital city of Canaan. Elkanah gave portions of meat that were to be sacrificed to Peninnah and her children but to Hannah, he gave a worthy or a double portion because "he loved" her. In my research, I found out that Hannah's name meant grace or favour. So every time someone called her name, they were prophesying that God was going to bless her in an unmerited, unexplainable fashion.

Hannah prayed to God for a child, and she vowed that if He granted her request, she would give him back to The Lord as a life-long Nazirite. A great definition of a Nazirite is one who is sanctified, separated, or consecrated to God.

Once God opened up the womb of Hannah and caused her to bring forth a son, she did as she vowed; she took her son to the temple to be raised by Eli the Priest. During the day that Samuel was handed over to the priest, Hannah prayed a powerful prayer in I Samuel 2:1-10. The first five verses say, "And Hannah prayed, and said, my heart rejoiceth in the Lord, mine horn is exalted in the Lord: my mouth is enlarged over my enemies; because I rejoice in thy salvation. There is none holy as the Lord; for there is none beside thee: neither is there any rock like our God. Talk no more so exceedingly proudly; let not arrogance come out of your mouth: for the Lord is a God of knowledge, and by him actions are weighed. The bows of the mighty men are broken, and they that stumbled are girded with strength. They that were full have hired out themselves for bread; and they that were hungry ceased so that the barren hath born seven, and she that hath many children is waxed feeble." Hannah gave a precious seed to God; she gave her first-born son, Samuel. As a result, he became a great prophet in Israel. The bible said not one of his words fell to the ground.

Parents who learn to understand godly encounters can tap into it and cause it to manifest in their lives, and that was who Hannah was. Parents must learn to take the extra mile in seeking what they want, be it child, transformation and redemption in the lives of their child/children who have gone wayward, or barrenness, and other reasons. Hannah was not just seeking a child, but a transformer, someone who will change the operations in the priestly order of Israel.

Reading through her prayer should give you an insight that something prompted her to ask God for that child; the then priests were not meeting up to the expectations of God in serving His people as it should be, so she now prayed for a child who will come from her womb and will not just change the lineage but set a new order according to the desire of God's heart. And she did just that, nurturing that child to her death, ensuring he lacked nothing and yearly providing him with a new priestly garment, always keeping her vow of ensuring that the order was kept; that was why in Samuel's dying days he asked the nation of Israel if he had collected or seized any of their property with force? Because His mother has served as a check to the life of her child and priest of Israel by ensuring he is well provided for, she gave the child and God blessed her womb with other siblings after Samuel.

If I may ask you parents, if God gave you that child to raise him to become the next Samuel of this generation, will you yield and submit to that request and demand? Will you permit that child to function as a priest for God as Hannah did? Parenting is not just imposing your own instructions, but equally understating and yielding to the instructions you heard from God pertaining to the life and destiny of that child. Hannah could have withheld Samuel from the Lord because no one heard the cry and yearning in her heart to

God aside from the priest of that time Eli, but she yielded to that.

Her influence was what Samuel had and used to become the greatest priest of Israel, oh what an honour for parents to realize that when they are models their wards listen to, their hearts can be at peace even if they were told of contrary reports against their child/children.

The influence of parents over their children or child might not be noticed in the beginning, but a time of reaping always comes when parents either smile in thanks to God and their labour or frown and weep in regret for not being part of their children's growth and development. So, when God gives you a child and you handle him/her well, he/she knows that if he gives your other children, you will train them as you had with that one. So, when he gives you one, it's because that's your capacity; when He gives you more, it is because he has given you the capacity to raise them as well, but how many parents are aware of this?

His command to go and multiply was not just in number but also in modelling and creating a pattern for all to see and live by; how blessed and glorious will it be when it is said that you as a parent created that pattern?

Moses – Jochebed (Exodus)

Moses is one of the greatest men God ever made. Known as the emancipator and lawgiver of Israel, he was also a scholar, soldier, statesman, and saint. He was one of the two men who were sent back from the otherworld to confer with Christ on the Mount of Transfiguration (Matt. 17:18). He wrote the first song in Scripture (Exod. 15:119), and in glory, they still sing the song of Moses. Only now it is muted as the great stanzas of that song awaken the echoes of the everlasting hills in "The song of the Lamb" (Rev. 15:3). Much of the credit for what he became must be given to his mother, Jochebed.

It's a known fact that "children are quivers/arrows in the hands of a warrior", but there are children of prophecy who have certain destinies tight to the surroundings of their birth, and we will see some here too.

Most mother's hearts are usually soft, and weaken when it comes to discipline but there is a reason for that; so also when it comes to risking a child they suffered in child bearing to deliver, they can go to any length to protect that child even at the expense of their lives. That was the scenario that surrounded Moses. The then Pharaoh gave a command that all the Israelites were to be killed upon birth but the two midwives defied that law; then he commanded again that any Israelite child given birth to or being below the age of 3 should be thrown into the River Nile; but Jochebed did not give in to this command and kept her child for a long time and was nurturing him with the other family members until it reached a point that they could not keep him again so had to take him to the Nile in hope that God will send a rescue; and that was the Pharaoh's daughter.

She went through that painful process until God used that scenario to bring the child into the hands of Pharaoh's daughter and back to her for upbringing until he reached the age of weaning. Even though she was paid to raise her child, that did not interest me much more what she was using those years she now freely had to do. She was imbibing the values and cultures of the Jewish tradition to an already Egyptian child, teaching him to know his roots and to realize that one day they must be delivered; so that by the time he was taken to the Palace, the transition and modeling had been completed − Egyptian child with a Jewish training and mindset. Our homes should be places where goodness and godliness are constantly taught and exemplified, even during a child's earliest days. For it is then that his soul's citadel must be stormed; it will be ten thousand times harder to capture later on.

Few women have had to raise a family in more difficult circumstances. The fact that a Moses, a Miriam, and an Aaron could come from a slave hut on the Nile says much about Jochebed's influence.

Hebrews 11:23 links the faith of Moses to the faith of his mother and father: "By faith, Moses, when he was born, was hidden for three months by his parents, because they saw he was a proper child; and they were not afraid of the king's commandment." The king's wrath was something to be reckoned with, but they discounted it because they feared the wrath of God far more. They made up their minds not to murder their child in cold blood just to comply with the tyrannical edict of a wicked king. God, in turn, honoured their faith.

The early years of training and teachings you give your child takes the deeper root ever, you are planting a seed that will not be uprooted, the moment you leave it blank and empty, it gives the enemy that opportunity and chance to plant his own, and believe me once he does you cannot gain control of your child again unless with the mercy of God. The planting might be in the word of God, time and attention, words from you, actions and things you believe in that he/she should equally do and many others, but they are all seeds. Jochebed had not left her baby alone in his ark. His sister Miriam watched over him.

The Jesuits used to say, "Give us a child until he's seven, and you can do what you like with him after that." We know that Jochebed would have agreed with them because she did a thorough job of training Moses.

Eventually the order came from the palace: "Send me Moses." As Jochebed kissed Moses goodbye, she probably said, "Remember what I've taught you, my son." Moses never forgot that he was a Hebrew. The universities of Egypt, the temptations of the palace, the lure of position, power, wealth, and the possibility of a worldly throne never erased his mother's training.

A time will come that you will be away from them, but you have planted a seed that will last in them, so, even if that child is misled or wayward, he/she will always remember those early stages. In such times, he/she will experience a nudging in his/her subconscious mind, and someday it will sprout out to the rescue of that child.

So how much time do you spare for your child? What value are you adding in those early stages and how productive will they become in your absence? What thoughts are you channelling towards that child in enhancing his/her growth? Likewise, when we commit our children to Christ, God still expects us to take all the prudent measures we can to shield them. He does not bless carelessness and lack of common sense.

All those things played out in Moses' life led to his captivity, when He saw an Egyptian beating an Israelite, all he registered was that this is one of me that is being treated like this, and he rushed to the scene and killed that Egyptian; though He left Egypt with an uncompleted process but all this could not have played out if his parents had not raised him in that light. Remember, what you give priority to is what you place value on.

Samson – Manoah's Child (Judges 13)

Few women of history show the strength of character and "spunk" of this Hebrew wife and mother from the twelfth century B.C. She was called like Sarah, Hannah and the Virgin Mary, to give birth to one of the great men of ancient times. But she models for modern women in more than just the courage of motherhood: Her spiritual qualities are a challenge to all who read the sacred Scriptures, men as well as women.

That's another child of promise. It's one thing for parents to understand prophecy and another for them to permit its flow and orchestration just as it is in the heart of God. Manoah and his wife never had a child, and when it was told to them by the angel that they are to bear a child, it sounds almost unbelievable.

But the mother believed the message of God's envoy (13:3,4). God did not give his notice of a child to Manoah, who would become the father of Samson, but to his wife, possibly because Manoah's faith in God's word was weaker than hers. It seems that Manoah found it harder to accept the idea that a son was finally coming to them after waiting so long. However, his wife did not dispute or raise any objections to the angel's announcement. That she told her husband all that had happened and all the angel had said is proof of the intensity of her faith in the Lord.

His parents understood the prophecy according to what the angel of God said; he was to be a Nazarene. *She accepted the (Nazirite) vows of holiness (13:4, 5, 13).* The Nazirites consecrated themselves to serve God, usually for a short period of time (Num. 6:5), because it was not easy to fulfil the restrictions demanded: drink neither wine nor beer; eat only kosher foods; never approach a dead body; do not cut your hair. Samson's mother agreed to keep these vows of a clean and dedicated life, even if her famous son should fail to do so.

She obeyed God's call to be a mother (13:24,25). From the uncertainties of conception to the pains of childbirth, motherhood can be a dangerous prospect. Childbearing was even more fearful in olden times before present-day medical knowledge and maternal and prenatal care. Rachel's tragic death at the birth of Benjamin, for example, was never forgotten by the Israelites (Gen. 35:18). But Samson was born just as the angel of the Lord had promised, and God gave him both a strong, healthy body and the power of the Holy Spirit. However, when the text says "he grew" it is clear that he reached full manhood due to his mother's care and guidance. He would "begin the deliverance of Israel from the Philistines, "a work that armies under Samuel and David would someday complete.

Even though they could not understand the orchestration in God's heart that had to do with that child; we can see that from his marriage to the Philistine lady. Though they made him understand He was a Nazarene whose assignment was to liberate, but they did not see the connection of him marrying the Philistine, because The Torah records many mixed marriages: Moses himself had two foreign wives; Judah had a Canaanite wife, Tamar; Joseph married an Egyptian, mother of the two tribes of Manasseh and Ephraim. But there was always the danger of the wife's pagan faith entering into the life of Israel. Thus Solomon was warned that foreign wives might "turn your hearts after their gods" (1 Kings 11:2).

But note that God could have used any occasion and circumstances to cause his mission/assignment to begin, but he has to use that of the marriage as it best suits his plan. And from then on, that opening caused unrest in the Philistines nation until his death. But to his parents, there could be other means not through marriage. Parents, perhaps two things God did or gave you over your children are: (i) being custodians and (ii) preservers and keepers and trainees to whom that child will belong, but there always comes a time that He will demand total control of that which He gave you as a trust in your custody; and when He demands, that day you seize to become custodians and He takes control.

The parents ensured that he lived just according to the word of the Lord, though in a few instances they tried to disrupt the plan, even though at the end there was no continuity in the lineage, but they rested well knowing that the child's destiny worked according to the plan they were given/told.

I wish I could talk a bit on continuity in family lineage to the third and fourth generation, but will not at the moment. So as a parent, how will you know that your child is a promised one? What did God tell you upon his/her birth and growth so far? Parents are spiritual beings raising spiritual beings to also raise spiritual beings in their day; because for every child the Lord gives in your care is on a mission to fulfil a desire in God's heart for his/her day.

Jesus – Mary (Mathew, Mark, Luke and John)

It is mothers who understand divine encounters to accept such responsibility as Mary did. Maybe, the day Mary found herself was not quite different from our own dispensation.

Mary resided in "her own house" in <u>Nazareth</u> in <u>Galilee</u>, possibly with her parents, and during her betrothal—the first stage of a <u>Jewish marriage</u>—the <u>angel</u> Gabriel announced to her that she was to be the mother of the promised <u>Messiah</u> by conceiving him through the Holy Spirit, and, after initially expressing incredulity at the announcement, she responded, "I am the handmaid of the Lord. Let it be done unto me according to your word." Joseph planned to quietly divorce her, but was told her conception was by the Holy Spirit in a dream by "an angel of the Lord"; the angel told him to not hesitate to take her as his wife, which Joseph did, thereby formally completing the wedding rites.

For every child the Lord gives, he/she is on a mission to fulfil and desire in God's heart for his day, and for the child Jesus the mission was to save the whole world from damnation and sin and restore them to the bosom of God. Due to the pressure of the society which Mary had to cope with, and perhaps Joseph taking time to accept who the child really was to become, made it a bit difficult but Mary who had an encounter with the angel will not permit her fate and belief to be moved. So when the child was born; she took her time to train and protect Him, so that in one scenario when at the temple, when the parents were looking for him, when they found him, he responded, "why are you looking for me, don't you know that I am supposed to be in my father's house?" and the scripture recorded that she kept it to herself. That's because she now realized that those words and encounters are beginning to form who the child was to be, and perhaps that prompted her to prophecies about the coming Saviour of the world, and perhaps it was at that moment that she was realizing what child she had actually been training or raising. People might argue that there was no record of his early stages of childhood which is true but he cannot just be raised by anyone, because he had parents that were mentioned. Which should tell us that those parents who now knew the prophecy surrounding him had to raise their child.

We later see instances in the scripture that she had to permit him to reveal his identity and not to perform miracles (the wedding at Cana) where he turned water to wine. Upon her request, though his answer was a bit contrary- "woman, why do you involve me? my hour has not yet come"(John 2:4). Apparently, she believed in her son's ability and not a way to show off, but to fulfil a need to the people he had come for; Jesus honoured that request not just because she was his mother but because of the manner in which she raised him. Children must understand that when parents notice a strong move of God upon them (you), they will always place demand in some cases or when demands arise, and that's because they believe in you not minding the timing.

Parents are usually supposed to be the first to believe in their children; and there is no record in the Bible which showed she ever doubted the course her son was on and did not even interfere, but stood with him to ensure his mission of becoming the saviour of the world was made manifest to the end. As awkward as it may sound when parents say to a child "I believe in you", it triggers a place and an awareness in that child to do what will please his/her parents and make them proud. Her influence over his life will not be taken for granted, but there can't be an interference with His God ordained mission. In such moments, all that a child requires from you parents is to know that he/she has your full support to help him/her in becoming that which he/she is destined to become. But when you interfere, a child is always broken between obeying and respecting you-his/her earthly parents or obeying the will of God which you are meant to help make him understand. Parents will forever remain custodians of generations coming through the loins of their children and family line, but will not be the orchestrators to what the child is to become; all they are meant to do is to help guide them in making the choice that goes in line with what his/her assignment is meant to be.

So rather than enforcing your own decision on them, why not work hand in hand with what they want to become? And that will only be successful when you as the parents actually know what God wants; and that will only be possible when you have discerned and know what destiny that child carries; once you do that, then there won't be need for you to enforce your own will against theirs.

Prayer is influence, and if parents don't pray over their children, they cannot have influence on that child. Looking at all these people mentioned, and how their lives turned out to be, that could only be possible and successful and made manifest as a result of the prayers offered by the parent before birth, after birth and during the growth, because it's in the place of prayer that you now believe who and what that child will become. It's only in the place of prayers that you begin to claim and trust God on how the destiny of your child should turn out to be according to prophecy; it's not when he /she is still a foetus and when given birth to that "fervent prayer ends", fervent prayer continues from when the child is born to when you successfully pass on the same baton to that child to run with it effectively until he exchanges that into his children's hands, and to the next generation. Only when you are sure that the baton is passed without any form of fault, then can you say you are a fulfilled parent.

I was privileged to perhaps be one of the closest grandsons to my grandfather, so that when he passed away, I could not imagine how to continue life without those moments when he woke up at mid night to pray, calling the names of all his children and grandchildren, I was not told this but I heard because I usually slept in his room whenever I went to the village; but in the course of time, I also noticed my mother doing that, from when I was a toddler till this moment, she wakes up in the night too and prays, for not just her children but also the entire lineage. So I told myself one time, at home you are secured, but out of home you need to stand on your feet…my grandfather passed the baton, my mother is ensuring she passes the same baton and I told myself several times I will have to receive the baton and pass it to my children also.

If they left a mark in our lives, why can't we do the same in our time? If we can have parents who will rise to that responsibility, you can imagine what generation will be raised in the coming years and dispensation. Jesus equally passed the baton to the twelve, who passed it onto another generation who kept passing it until we have become benefactors of it, the question is will we be willing to pass the baton? Will it be as we received from those who handed it down to us?

Susanna Wesley – John and Charles Wesley

Susanna Wesley was the mother of John and Charles Wesley. She was married to Reverend Samuel Wesley, who was an Anglican Rector.

Susanna educated all of her children at home and made time to instil faith and prayer into each one. The children were taught not only to pray daily but also to give themselves in service to others and the Lord.

Charles Wesley, Susanna's youngest child became very accomplished, although his memory is often overshadowed by his brother, John. Charles left the Anglican Church and travelled extensively with his brother until his health began to deteriorate. He is remembered for the many hymns he wrote, which today are considered classics, like "Christ the Lord is Risen Today", "Oh, for a Thousand Tongues to

Sing", and "Hark, the Herald Angel Sing." Charles' greatest gift to Methodism was his hymns. These hymns are sung all over the world by various Christian denominations. He wrote over 7000 hymns; publishing 4,500 and leaving the rest in manuscript form which were later published in his honour. He accomplished his personal mission of massive song writing by finishing three songs per week. When he attended Oxford University, he founded the Holy Club. The participants of this club were called Methodist because of their methodical practices. Later, his brother John became the leader of the group. John was special to his family because he escaped a near death situation as a five-year-old. John was trapped on the second story of the family's home which was on fire. John escaped through a window. His family lost everything in the fire but they were grateful that no one was injured. His parents said that John was "a brand plucked from the burning." John's mother came to the realization that her son's life was spared for a specific purpose and she paid close attention to his spirituality in an effort to shape his destiny. Like all the Wesley children, John's busy day began well before dawn. He was expected to read from the Bible, say the Lord's prayer, recite Bible verses, say a prayer from the Book of Common Prayer, and pray for his family members. Once all that was done, he could attend family devotions. Every Thursday, his mother spent an hour with each child. She instructed him to walk in the ways of Christ. John took his mother's advice, traveling on horseback, preaching the gospel sometimes two or three times a day. He formed many societies, established many churches, commissioned preachers, administered charities, superintended schools and orphanages. He married at the age of forty-eight to a widow, Mary Vazeille, and had no children. He died peacefully, at age 88 after a short illness, leaving 541 itinerant preachers under the name "Methodist".

Abigail Adams

It is hard to believe that Mrs. Adams did not receive a formal education but her family had a collection of books in their personal library and her mother taught her how to read. Mrs. Adams was no stranger to the church or politics as she came from a consistent line of clergymen and politicians. In 1825, her son, John Quincy Adams became the sixth President of the United States. When he was ten years old, she allowed him to go overseas with his father for over seven years. His father was in diplomatic roles in Paris, Amsterdam, St. Petersburg and England. When he was 14 years old, he accompanied Francis Dana to St. Petersburg and served him as a translator and secretary. Therefore, John became very familiar with politics at an early age. When Mrs. Adams sent letters to her son, she often included scriptures, prayers and motherly encouragement. While he was in law school, he fell in love with a pretty lady and his mother persuaded him to postpone marriage until he could afford having a wife and family. John agreed and called the relationship off. This action showed that he was obedient to his mother. I believe she was prompted by the Holy Spirit to groom him in a fashion so that he would be prepared to lead one of the greatest countries in the world. Her letters are featured in many books and have been placed on exhibition often. For example, Mrs. Adams apparently could not be present at her husband's inauguration, so she wrote an inspiring letter that included a stately prayer. "And now, O Lord, my God, thou hast made thy servant ruler over the people. Give unto human understanding heart, that he may know how to go out and come in before this great people; that he may discern between good and bad. For who is able to judge this thy so great a people? 'were the words of a royal sovereign; and not less applicable to him who is invested with the chief magistracy of a nation, though he wear not a crown, nor the robes of royalty …My thoughts and my meditations are with you, though personally absent; and my petitions to Heaven are, that thethings which make for peace may not be hidden from your eyes. That you may be enabled to discharge them with honor to yourself, with justice and impartiality to your country, and with satisfaction to this great people, shall be the daily prayer of your *A.A.*"

Her letter may not be grammatically sound but it was a powerful example of love and devotion.

She passed the same devotion down to her beloved son who made history by becoming the first President, whose father also held the same office. President George W. Bush is the second President to attain this great accomplishment.

Pearline Black

Rev. Barry C. Black serves our nation as Chaplain of the United States Senate. Appointed by former President, Bill Clinton in June 2003, Rear Admiral Black (Ret.), served in the United States Navy for more than 27 years, ending his distinguished career as the Chief of Navy Chaplains. He is the 62nd chaplain of the Senate. The first Chaplain was appointed in 1789. This is a life-time appointment. Black was dedicated as a baby to the Lord by his mother, Pearline Black. He recalls that he and his family would be in church every time the doors were opened. When his mother was pregnant with him, she asked God to bless her unborn child. Black said he had never wanted to be anything else but a minister.

Black's father died at an early age, leaving his Godly mother to raise him and his brothers and sisters. Raising a large family alone, Mrs. Black, found that the church offered that supportive environment she needed to supplement her children's spiritual and social growth.

He recalls his mother giving him and his siblings a nickel for scriptures they had memorized. He said she had to change her reward system by putting him on a flat rate because he was "breaking the bank." Mrs. Black taught her eight children the importance of God and education as the way to a better life without poverty.

As a result of his mother's guidance, Black's life is a blessing to many. He shares the gospel and love of Jesus Christ with others. Black opens each Senate session with prayer and offers spiritual guidance to members of the Senate, their families and their staff. On occasion, Chaplain Black is called upon to advise senators on moral issues. He attended two schools of higher education; Pine Forge Academy in Pennsylvania and Oakwood College in Alabama. He later became a pastor in North Carolina, where he met a group of sailors who had driven miles to attend his church service because they were not satisfied with the spiritual nourishment they were getting on their naval base.

This prompted Black to join the Navy and become a chaplain. He rose to the ranks of Rear Admiral, commanding all the chaplains of the Navy, Marines and Coast Guard.

Rev. Black is the first African-American, and the first military chaplain to hold the office of chaplain to the United States Senate. He is married and has three sons.

Be it as a parent or single, God has equally willed you with that ability and strength to raise that child. All he wants you to realize is that the child is on a mission, and he needs you to accomplish that mission.

Being a role model, is one of the things children expect from their parents, that every time they do whatever they do that they will do it in such a way that the children will be inspired to be able to do the same; and doing that makes it easier for the parents to expect the same from their children, so parents must first become examples of the lives they wish their wards will live before that larger society, like in Mahatma Gandhi's words "be the change that you want to see in the world".

I watched the video Fela Durotoye did on modelling, where he gave an instance of a parent who lived in an estate where the road has dual carriage, and his house is on the right side of the road. If he was to come out and do the right thing, he would have literally needed to go down the road and then turn back at the roundabout and come towards the gate, but since everyone does it that way he also had to; but don't forget the words of St. Augustine "right is right even if no one is doing it, wrong is wrong even if everyone is doing it"; so once he comes out he checks to see if the road is clear, then he takes the turn the opposite way through the gate to make it shorter; this has been a practice for years until he decides that he is going to be a **role model.** So, he is taking his Son for a haircut the day after he takes this value on a Sunday, ready for the next week. As he comes out that Sunday evening, of course there is very little traffic, and he makes the turn to go the right way and his son shouts 'Daddy where are you going? you are going the wrong way, and tears fell down his eyes, because he realized that all the while he had been showing his son the wrong thing, but because his son believed the best in his dad, he believed what he was doing was right whereas he's been modelling in the wrong path; and just like Charles F Keterring said "Every father should remember that one day his son will follow his example (s) instead of his advice". Like Fela said (paraphrased) "if everyone did what you did as a parent, would we have a better or worst nation?" If everyone says the kind of things you say, would we have a happier nation, a better nation, or a more prosperous nation?

Fela Durotoye shared the story of a university he went to once, which had about 5000 people that were there to listen to him and he asked them a question, how many of you love your parents? And almost all hands went up; then he asked How many think their parents are heroes and role models for them in their career, and would like their career to go through the path their parents had, to his surprise in less than 30 seconds only 6 people had their hands up. "The choice of who you love is an emotional decision, but the choice of a role model is a sensitive and intellectual decision; your children may love you because you are their parent (s), but will not necessarily choose you as their role model because of the fact that you are their parents." – Fela D.

So being a role model to your children has to be a conscious decision you need to take as a parent, be someone they admire, not just look up to but find in you someone who they will like to be. So how do you intend to be a role model?

Chapter 4

The Teacher, For Educational And Moral Child Upbringing

The Bible says, "train a child in the way he should go [and in keeping with his individual gift or], and when he is old he will not depart from it. (Proverbs 22:6 – AMP] So, the shortest distance between a problem and a solution is the distance between your knees and the floor.

Parents should spend time with their children

Family is the first mission field God gave to every parent. And in God's designed plan, he did not specify that it is the responsibility of the mother alone, but a collective one. So let me add, that if the child goes wayward, the parents should take responsibility.

In the heart of God, there has always been a pattern of parenting that He desires to be used in raising and modelling/training children. But it seems along the line, the pattern has been distorted leading to a lot of errors being experienced in our day. One of the things this book tries to address is that children are world changers for whose propagation God wants to use, on his behalf, the parents. The psalmist also wrote: "**Sons are a heritage from the Lord, children, a reward from him. Like arrows in the hands of a warrior are sons born in one's youth. Blessed is the man whose quiver is full of them. They will not be put to shame when they contend with their enemies in the gate" Psalms 127:2-5 NIV**

And a poet Shelley R. Davis also shared from one of his poem,

I sit and wonder where time goes

we try our best to teach them right,

as times change and our children grow,

We love them with all our might.

It's not easy to raise a child

at times, we don't know what to do

we weren't given any instructions

It's a challenge that's all new.

Our children are our lives

and our most important goal,

to love and to guide them

and to place them in life's role.

Our children are our future

and time will only tell

the job we've done as parents

and if we've done it well....

Definition: Training means discipline in order to equip one with ability or quality so that it improves on the quality of the life of the individual in all facets of life: physically, mentally, emotionally and spiritually. Thus it means that training a child has to conform to the above. Who takes responsibility for this training or instruction or teaching the child? Certainly, there are different people along the ladder constructed by the society that must shoulder the responsibility.

The Hebrew verb translated "train" as channak and has become part of the contemporary Hebrew terminology for learning. Today, chinuch means "education", and mekhanekh alludes to an "educator". The Hebrew word for "child" is na'ar, and can refer to the age between childhood and maturity.

We thus can say that, "training is an early education given to a child by an educator (which is mostly administered by the parent or teacher etc.) to bring up the child in a manner or way to make him/her a responsible individual with a unique and wonderful character/behaviour in the society where he/she lives or the society at large".

Traditional Methods Of Training

We will now consider some traditional ways in which children are trained and their significance/benefits.

The Mwaghavul Tradition (Nigeria)

For a male child, he is expected to wake up as early as possible, around 6am to prepare to go to the farm and help the father, while with peers he learns to compete on the farm and also to look after the flocks. The daughter is expected to clean all the compound in order to ensure that the vicinity is clean and well-arranged as well as later on join the male and other family members on the farm. The male child is also expected to be close to the father, to get advice and education about life in general, and on how to be a good and responsible father in his own family (later in life). The daughter on the other hand will get closer to the mother to also get pieces of advice and education on how to nurture and train the children in a godly way as well as learn maintenance, good conduct and behaviour and how to live with fellow women in her own house and her in-laws', and so on.

The aim of all these training is to help the child learn respect, integrity, responsibility and independence.

The Hausa Tradition (Nigeria)

The child is expected to go through the stages of education: The normal school and The Arabic school. The child is monitored closely i.e. by questioning to ensure that the child understands all that he/she is being taught in order to build his/her IQ, and this helps the child to be responsible later on in life, both in the house and society. Another thing a child is taught to be conversant with is the time to go for prayers and the individual time for personal prayers. The child is also taught to read and memorize the Quran and the application from childhood to when he/she is an adult.

All this training builds the child towards looking after the home or starting a business of his/her own with the knowledge acquired from these two basic forms of education as well as respect for religion, prayer and the Quran.

In Ngas Tradition

In those days, children are backed using the skin. So, from the age of ten, the male child begins to go to the farm with the father and also learns to rear flocks, and the female also cleans the environment and then follow the mother to fetch firewood. The male child is also taught how to hunt from the age of fifteen. But from eighteen, is taught how to be independent by looking for dogs to sell to earn a living. In terms of education, parents also contribute the best they can to educate the children to have the white man knowledge.

The training helps the child from childhood to the age of maturity to be independent and then struggle for themselves to earn a living and means of survival.

Igbo Tradition

The aspect of training to be discussed or looked at in this tradition is from Abia State of Nigeria, and from the tribe of Ngwa which is the dominant tribe in Abia state.

The family setting is always in a large setting or stratum. In this tradition, there is high respect for the elderly: calling a senior male or brother- dede, and senior female or sister- da'a; as well as using two hands to greet the elderly signifies part of being respectful as well.

The child is taught to tell the truth, and work very hard as well as attend Church activities to worship God. There is also a bond of unity that brings families and individuals together i.e. Ama; they also engage in building houses and clearing bushes for another member of the community which helps for people to come together.

In the case of which the father/mother of one dies, the children of the deceased automatically call the next elderly person in the family 'father' or 'mother'.

In most cases, the child does not belong to the family alone, but to his/her community, so that when the child misbehaves, he/she is immediately cautioned before reporting the offense to his\her biological parents.

The training helps the children to be united i.e. through the communal work they engage in; it helps the individual become responsible i.e. by being monitored closely; it also helps such children become conscious of who he\she is; as well as gives you an identity whenever you meet someone who your place or through your behaviour and character; it also helps the child become truthful i.e. through the Godly training received at home from parents and elderly ones.

In Yoruba Tradition

The Yoruba tradition lays more emphasis on the religious aspect of child training, but both parents are involved in that. So the child is first trained in God's way, and not always allowed to roam about but to be engaged in Church activities so as to be watched closely in order to not go astray or deviate.

After the family, the child is guided on the kind of friends he/she is to have and keep because that helps the child in respecting the elderly ones. The male and female children are supposed to prostrate and kneel respectively at the time of greeting, it has no age limit so it's meant for all age groups.

For women, while growing up they are expected to be close to the mother to be taught basic things pertaining womanhood and motherhood; the male child on the other hand, goes close to the father to be taught about fatherhood, he is also informed or intimated on the family inheritance. This is done so that the child should know that the inheritance given is not to be sold but preserved for the next generations. In most cases, the male child is handed the inheritance.

The importance of this practice to the child starts when the child begins school, by being taught to be intelligent i.e. carrying their books and engaging in personal studies after school hours. He/she is then taught to guard/protect his/her school property to avoid being punished/disciplined.

Sometimes, children are promised good things to make them study hard. In most cases, the father is the one who chairs the family devotion by reading Bible scriptures and then praying too.

All these, enhance high rate of discipline, respect and telling the truth when wrong so as to avoid being disciplined, but as well be commended and praised, most fathers read and emphasize on the book of Proverbs 3, "My child, remember my teachings and instructions...a long and prosperous life"1&2.

Berom Tradition

The eldest son is respected by other family members, and he also administers discipline on the others when they misbehave. Parents also discipline, but he does that most of the time. When a child errs, he's punished and sometimes denied food as part of being disciplined.

At other times, there are public punishments for any individual that defies constituted authority within the community; it is done by being lashed/beaten by the Sunday school teacher or most senior of the male adult. The public punishment is led by a panel that first unravels the root of the matter before stating the kind of punishment to be given for the crime/offense committed.

In farming activities, the father leaves first to begin work; the male follows too, and does most of the farming work while the father sings songs to boost their morale and answer questions asked by the male children. Later, the female children join them in the farm together with the mother with food and drinks where they also participate in the farming work too.

All these help the child be a better person; learn how to build his/her home, and also in choosing a hardworking and suitable life partner. If a child is hard working, it is noticed not just by family members but even the community, so that, if an opportunity for employment comes, such a person is considered or nominated by the community; it also leads to the children respecting their parents which builds love and unity amongst the family unit.

It is obvious then, that as a result of accepting westernization, there is a wide margin/gap created between the traditional pattern of training and the western culture of training children.

It implies therefore, that the parents, elders, community leaders and religious leadership have roles in training the child, but parents have the key role of training the child/children, because it is their solemn responsibility (Prov. 22:6), all others give a helping hand to help mould the child to be a good person, as well as instruct, teach and discipline the child in the path of growth. One would dare to say that only a few are able to do that, because it is not a small commitment; its demands are great and tedious.

I attended a programme some time ago, and while I was waiting for the programme to start, a mother came in with her two little children and she was teaching them how to memorize some verses in the Bible. I marvelled and said to myself, how many of our parents still have the time to train their children this way? How many parents and those listed above are ready to dedicate their time to sit and know some of the things these children need as well as the challenges they face on a daily basis? It would be a hazard to say that maybe only a few are able to do it, because it is not a small commitment, its demands are great and tedious.

Training is also a process that continues from childhood to adulthood and to marriage, because that is the stage that the child sets his/her home. Students of Child development emphasize the critical value for the first three years of life. Moses wrote *"these commands that I give you today are to be on your hearts. Impress them on your children. Talk about them when you sit at home and when you walk along the road, when you lie down and when you get up"*. And Jesus said, *"Let the little* **children** *come to me, and do not hinder them, for the kingdom of heaven belongs to such as these"*. The bible encourages parents to be faithful in rearing their children (B.S.F 1960, 2004, 2013) because as the children grow older, they begin to assume responsibilities that are new or already known.

A father holding the hands of his small baby,
learning to walk

(Source:Picturesque)

The Torah instructs parents to teach the word of God to their children, and their children after them, (Deuteronomy 4:9; 6:7). The Talmud reveals the father's significance in teaching his son by saying: "the father is bound in respect of his son, to circumcise…teach him Torah and teach him a craft; (The Talmud Kiddushin 29a). Teaching begins at an early stage. From a Hebraic perspective, training a child is more than consistently instructing a child in right and wrong. Every child is born with a distinct personality, certain inner gifts and ability that are as unique as that child's individual fingerprints. As a child grows from infancy through the early stages of becoming a young adult, the parents are to discern the inclinations and possible gifts within the child's personality and key/support the gifts he/she has to help the child to fulfil his or her appointed destiny (Perry Stone 2009).

Moses was a good example of this, given birth by Hebrew parents but spent most of his 40 years in the Egyptian court/palace, the mightiest nation of his day as a prince, "yet he turned his back on his privileges and identified with his own greatly despised people". He received the best secular education possible for a person of his day; however, it was in his own home and from a slave mother that he received his most important lesson till the age of three (3). The influence of a godly parent's life and teaching cannot be underestimated even when the parents do not see the results in their own time (BSF 1960, 2004, 2013), which implies that when a student/child is trained well, he/she becomes like his/her teacher/parent. The Bible tells us in Ephesians 6:4, "parents, do not treat your children in such a way as to make them angry, instead bring them up with Christian discipline and instructions" GNV.

As a parent, how have you denied your child the right and opportunity of going close to God? Is it through your busy activities? Refusing the child to do the will of God? Or ignorance? The Bible tells us "Jesus said, let the little children come to me and do not stop them, because the kingdom of God belongs to such as these" Matthew 19:14, GNV. There are times you have to take the same risk like Abraham (Genesis 21), because it might be a test. And maybe, many parents have failed that test. The time you spend teaching them what to do and what they should know has a lot of impact. Moses had a tangible time with his parents during his first three (3) years, that is why he was able to stand for his people rather than the Egyptians (Exodus 2:9-10). David and Solomon were another example; David had to train Solomon on how to be a good king (1 Kings 2:1-9). I believe no parent would want to be like Eli who could not train his children in the right manner, and their ending was bad. Jeroboam was another example; he was the King that led the children of Israel to sin (1 Kings 12:26 – 13:6 and 15:34)

This implies therefore, that Christian parents particularly are supposed to be examples not only in the house and society, but even to unbelievers, and that can only be done, seen and experienced by the manner in which your children are trained, because "charity begins at home". So, parents are you such an example?

Chapter 5

Strategies of Training Children

There are several ways on how to train a child to become a responsible adult/person. Below are some of the areas of human intervention in which children can be trained to become useful people in their later life.

Israel's article of faith, commonly known as the *Shema* declares:

Hear, O Israel: The Lord our God is one. Love the Lord your God with all your heart and with all your soul and with all your strength. These commandments that I give you today are to be upon your hearts. Impress them on your children. Talk about them when you sit at home and when you walk along the road, when you lie down and when you get up. Tie them as symbols on your hands and bind them on your foreheads. Write them on the door frames of your house and on your gates.

Deuteronomy 6:4-9 NIV

Harold, in his book: Train a child and be glad you did, says that: 'we parents teach our children in three ways; first and perhaps the most basic, is by our example; second, we teach by attitudes, which develops emotional response in our children; third, by our words'. (Harold J Sala, 1978)=

By Example

If you were to group together, parents and their children in one room, within an hour, you would likely be able to know who belongs with whom. The old saying 'the apple doesn't fall far from the tree is an understanding at best. Truth is that children learn how to behave, act and deal with life situations first and foremost by watching their parents. If a mother is constantly yelling and screaming at others, or she treats people with no respect, her children are likely to do the same. Likewise, if a father does not lift a finger to help with housework, chances are high that his own sons [and daughters] will grow up believing that this is how people are supposed to act. If as parents you consider your life with that of children for a moment, you will see that they have learned virtually everything from you.

A child being taught how to obey
instructions by his mother

(Source: Picturesque)

When children are young, they are most often parents' pleasers as they delight in following their examples to do simple things, such as putting their dish in the sink, or saying please and thank you to others. But as they get older and their interactions become more widespread, they become living mirrors of the behaviour they see of who they spend the most time with. Sadly, when parents behave badly which is often the case these days, they are likely to raise children that behave badly as well. The children are now accustomed to the 'do as I say', not as 'what I do is being watched by mum and dad intently'. They are learning to do things in the same manner at a young age. They hear you lying to your spouse, they see you cheating, are witnessing you drinking, smoking and engaging in unhealthy habits.

The same is true when it comes to hard-work. Children watch how hard their parents work and develop their work ethics from their parents. If you want your child to be successful in life, it is important that you show them first-hand that the key to success is hard work and dedication. Therefore, leading by example doesn't need words, the lessons that you teach your children by doing things the right way in their presence are far more long- lasting than the lessons you preach but don't actually adhere to yourself.

Allowing the child to make some decisions and choices helps a lot, but when he/she does that, he/she then needs your directives/guidance/help on the benefit/danger of making such choices/decisions.

By doing that, the child grows with the knowledge of differentiating between negative and positive choices/decisions. Allowing the child to take your responsibility at times (i.e. knowing that the child is capable) as a mother or father also aids the child later on in life when in position of authority etc., knowing that he/she has assumed such while still growing up, which can help scare away discouragement, timidity, fear and low self-esteem, when meeting their other peers.

"Children live what they learn, if a child lives with criticisms he/she learns to condemn, if a child lives with hostility he/she learns violence, if a child lives with ridicule he/she learns to be shy, if a child lives with encouragement he/she learns confidence, if a child lives with praise he/she learns to appreciate, if a child lives with fairness he/she learns justice, if a child lives with security he/she learns faith, if a child lives with approval he/she learns to like himself/herself, if a child lives with acceptance and friendship he/she learns to love the world." [Dorothy Law Nolte] (Zig Ziglar, 2001)

So, parents are the first example to the child before the society at large so if as a father or mother you cannot be an example to your children at home, then you need to look at who you are in the public again.

Parents are first to be spiritual beings raising another set of spiritual beings; that is to say as spiritual beings, you are always alert of any slight change in the environment of your child. "irrespective of your working condition"; parenting is not easy but is worth it. Because when you do your homework well, you have just sown a seed that you will reap the benefit of in due time.

My mother, after years of not buying us clothes, still knows the ones that are new and the ones old, so if you have any in your possession that she knows not, trust me, she will ask questions. That's how parenting is, knowing what kind of character and attitude your child has is different from the one he/she learnt from home or you, knowing how he talks and what has changed in that regard, what he/she listens to different from what he is used to listening; the moment he begins to develop a new character/behaviour than the one you know him with, asides just taking cognisance you need to take measures to stop that from growing; because what you can't stop from the onset, you will have to contend with later on.

In the house, I literally stopped the younger ones from listening and singing secular songs, so they are always careful to not attempt it in my absence, and any who tries to will be reported to me, why am I doing that? Teaching them to know that their bodies are temples of God, and where the spirit of God dwells/resides, another alternative spirit cannot live. Now with that consciousness, they will sing songs that they believe and know edifies them and their relationship with God. What made it possible for me to achieve that is because I don't sing and they have never heard me sing such kind of songs.

By Attitudes

In a world filled with negativity, violence and suffering, a positive attitude can make life more manageable. A good attitude enables you to develop the strength to deal with life's challenges. So, when children develop a positive attitude early in life, positive thinking becomes a habit that can ease the pressure associated with growing up.

Parents often forget that children aren't born with a built-in sense of respect for others. While each child has a different personality, all children need to be taught to be respectful. From birth, children learn to manipulate their worlds to get their needs met as this is natural, but it's your job as parents to teach them respectful ways.

Your job is to teach them to be able to function in the world, this means teaching them to behave respectfully towards others. We see children and teens arguing with adults [or ignoring them out-rightly], using foul language, ill-mannered and disrespectful. This means that you have to work hard as parents to teach the children the right attitude to respond to, otherwise, it will not only affect the child but also you as the parent. Ethical, moral values should be taught at home from the beginning, because they are morally absolute. With a solid character base to build on, your children can be successful in life.

By Words

As parents, our children should trust our words. Children need us to keep our words, i.e. do what you say you will do. Not doing so makes the child doubt your words. Example is telling your child that he/she will not eat for an offense, and then later giving the child the food. The next time the child does something else and you say the same word, they will tell themselves after all, they won't act or do what they said. Or promising the child a gift or something to encourage that child and not keeping to that promise. Lack of keeping to your promises/words as a parent makes the child ignore your words/authorities/commands; but keeping them will make your child trust and live to abide by them, leading the child to see the need to teach his/her children in the near future.

As parents, you should know that whatever you do good or bad, your child grows up to learn and practice that because he/she thinks and sees that as part of life and training [either positive or negative]. If children do the right thing, you commend and encourage them, as well as discipline them when you realize/notice that they are going the wrong path. But if you ignore all their behaviours when you are supposed to correct/caution them, you spoil them.

Now children also feel happy when they see you going wrong and talk to you, and see you listening to them and adhering to what they say or notice about you. When you appreciate them for that, it makes them happy and they find it easy to do what you tell them; but not accepting what they tell you when they noticed you are wrong will cause them to either ignore or disobey your warning and correction of them. It pays when you as a parent know that no one is above correction and heeding to what they say to you, so they can also love to obey your word/correction which brings mutual understanding and bonds the love of both of you.

Children need special care, not by nannies, uncles, aunties, and grandparent's etc. But from the parents because, what they learn growing up is what they grow up to live by. That is why Proverbs tells parents and none other to train the child in the way he should go and when he/she grows, it will not depart from their memory [Proverbs 22:6]. A lack in their training, brings a lot of trouble to you and the family. You need to give your children the best so that when they are weak, they will be enabled to climb the ladder of life to the top, in times of discouragement they will be strengthened to face challenges as they come. A child trained to depend on God will always grow to love and trust God, so children need you to train them.

Dr. Harold J Sala said "parents are the most important teachers a child will ever have". It follows therefore to say that being a parent is one of the last holdout of the amateurs. To drive a car, operate a cub radio, be a plumber, or practice medicine, you must be licensed, indicating that you may have a certain level of training and expertise in performing that function, but when it comes to being a parent, no professional training or expertise is required. It's easy to become a parent, but hard to parent". (Harold J Sala, 1978)

It is evident that for parents to be effective in the vineyard of the Lord, they must first be effective workers in the home. What good is it to any man or woman, if they are out saving souls but their home is in ruins? The scripture says, **he must be able to manage his own family well and make his children obey him with all respect. For if a man does not know how to manage his own family, how can he take care of the church of God?** 1Timothy 3:4-5 (Good News Bible)

In training children, parents must be humble, sincere and truthful to their children. Confessing their failures to their children and being realto them. They should know and stick to the word of God, and make sure they have and keep friends that will help them maintain their good standard and not ruin them.

Parents must also be united in the training of their children and avoid the use of abusive words on the child. It is one of the responsibilities of parents to know their children because, it is from that you get to know their moods and through God-given wisdom know what to do, but when you do not know your child, you can hardly tell what is happening to his/her life. Your child needs you now, not later, tomorrow or when you have the time, they need you at all times. And when training your child/children, do not always let any unwholesome talk come out of your mouth, but only what is helpful for building others up.

And one of the major roles God has given parents in raising children is the ability to speak and make it become. So when a parent speaks carelessly over a child's life, most especially abusively or through careless utterances, it comes to pass;

and when a parent equally speaks consciously over a child it also comes to pass.

When parenting, communication differs between that of a child and that of an adult. If you are honest as a parent, there are few things that you will identify in the life of your children that you find in your life; one single word that is a comprehensive definition and a practical explanation of what a parent is supposed to do and say every moment and day throughout the life of a child is meant to be representative.

Parents must know that they are representatives of the message, method and character of the king, because they are put to make the invisible king visible in the lives of their children. So anytime you exercise parental authority, God makes his invisible plan visible in the lives of children, which means whenever you exercise such authority it must be a beautiful picture of the authority of God.

So as a parent, if your eyes ever see and your ears ever hear the sin, weakness and failure of your children, it's never an accident, hassle, never an interruption, it's always GRACE, because God loves those children and as an act of his love has placed them in a family of faith and he will reveal the need of those children to you so you can be a tool of their rescue and restoration.

Paul Tripp in one of his messages made it clear that "the family is not meant to be comfortable, the family is meant to be transformational"; hopelessness is the doorway to parental hope, because only when you begin to believe that it's not by the force of your personality, the volume of your voice, by logic of your argument, by the scariness of your punishment that your child will change, but by divine grace that you change the way you parent.

Parents must realize that they are not the agents of change, but are ambassadors of the one who changes, you don't have to think that you can do what he alone can do, God holds the power of change. There are moments that parents have to ask themselves what God is doing and how they can be part of what he is doing in the lives of their children. Unless you come to parenting with the mentality of a representative, recognizing your own areas of weaknesses, failures and inability, but recognizing what God is able to do through you as you represent him; if you don't carry that with you, you will turn God given moments of ministry into moments of anger- Paul Tripp. Because you will now personalize what is not personal. At such moments it now becomes about you not the assignment you were given anymore and when you personalize it, it distorts the way that you are going to handle them.

When you personalize things that are not personal you become adversarial in your response, it won't be you for your children but you against your children

So from all these characters we have considered, we can come to the conclusion that the following are the roles of parents:

1. Parents are instructors:

    They teach their children the ways of Christ and the ways of the world. For example, many children know scriptural verses, Christian songs, etc. because the parents taught them. As they grow, they influence them to live by the principles of God. They teach them the ways of the world by instructing them to stay away from drugs, alcohol and sex outside of marriage. In fact, if there is a way the book of Proverbs can be the first book now henceforth parents must use it as guide, then there won't be need for shouting, raising hands out of anger and so forth on any child. But that can only be done the moment the child reaches that age of understating.

2. The mother is a Nurse

    When a Godly mother breast feeds a baby, she is giving that child more than milk; she is giving her child a part of herself. As the child gazes into its mother's eyes, the spirit of God may be imparted. When a child is sick and cranky, especially at night, a mother has to lovingly nurse her child back to health. Godly mothers are known for 'praying through' until the power of God change the adverse situation facing her or her child.

3. Parents are compassionate

I Kings 3:17 & 18 records that there were two roommates who had given birth to newborn babies. One of the women rolled over and crushed her baby to death. The bible says that at midnight, this woman switched babies with the woman she was sharing the room with. When the mother was going to breastfeed her child, she discovered that the child sleeping next to her was dead.

Immediately, she knew that the dead child did not belong to her. However, her roommate insisted that the living child was hers. Therefore, they took the matter to King Solomon who after hearing both testimonies decided to cut the baby in half. However, the bible says in I Kings 3:26, "Then spake the woman who's the living child unto the king, for her bowels yearned upon her son, and she said, O my lord, give her the living child, and in no wise slay it. But the other said, let it be neither mine nor thine, but divide it." The woman whose son was alive portrayed the characters and virtues of a Godly mother.

Most fathers, don't really show their love as the mothers do, perhaps because the mother tends to be the weaker vessels/cells and have to express theirs openly; but I can assure you that the compassion in the hearts of parents is higher, in the midst of that silence they can break due to emotions that cannot be physically seen or experienced. Even David, was compassionate to his son Absalom, whom though committed an act of treason, but from that place of compassion he still hopes that he will come back to realize and change his mind, that he told them to deal gently with the young lad Absalom (2

Samuel, 18:5) that's to tell you how the heart of a father can be.

4. Parent are personal consultants

Mothers mostly know what to say at the right time and at the moment you need to hear it. Also, a mother's words have a way of staying with you throughout your lifetime. Have you ever heard someone say, "My mother used to say…?"

Mothers are the bedrock of any society. For example, I found a story that 'drives my point home': "Some years ago, executives of a greeting-card company decided to do something special for Mother's Day. They set up a table in a federal prison, inviting any inmate who desired to send a free card to his mom. The lines were so long, they had to make another trip to the factory to get more cards. Due to the success of the event, they decided to do the same thing on Father's Day, but this time no one came. Not one prisoner felt the need to send a card to his dad. Many had no idea who their fathers even were. What a sobering illustration of a dad's importance to his children." Mothers should be appreciated every day, all day; especially a Godly mother!

In another insistence, the fathers mostly use few words, but in those few words they will share with the child a pool of wisdom and insight that if the child uses it wisely it becomes of great benefit to him.

Chapter 6

Life of Parenting A Child With Physical Disability

The birth of a child is a sign of faith and hope, prompting expectations of continuity and perpetuation. The mere existence of the newborn, the baby's traits and appearance, are usually a source of pride.

Around the globe, disability is still viewed in terms of a tragedy. A common perception of society behind this scenario is that it is not viable for a special child to be happy or enjoy a good quality of life. Parents find themselves different because their child is not normal. Many negative emotions flood into parents' minds when they observe their child getting social attention because of abnormality.

Raising a child with special needs often has negative effects on both relationships within the family and interactions with extra-familial people. Within the family, strained husband-wife and parent-child relationships are very common. According to Dobson et al. (2001) parents of children with disability undergo the period of grieving which is similar to that of bereavement. Parents grieve for the 'death' of the perfect child who existed in their minds.

Universal parental perceptions include seeing children as developing. Usually, some parents identify their children's condition as a temporary or passing circumstance, and perceive a disability as God's punishment. Parents' perceptions on the nature of a disability may differ to some point, based on their cultural ethics, educational level and past experiences.

All parents have plans and expectations for their children, often imagining future scenarios and the child's advances. The child's success is perceived as the parents' achievement. When a handicapped child is born, all expectations and hopes are dashed. It is difficult to perceive this child as a continuation of the parents' life.

The child is no source of pride – rather a source of great disappointment. Parents of physically handicapped/disabled children undergo a difficult and painful process involving a revision of their views and expectations. They are obliged to adapt to the knowledge that all their hopes and plans for the future must change.

There is no tested way to help parents avoid the shock and pain that accompany exposure of their child's handicap/disability. This is precisely why it is necessary to try and prevent any exacerbation and aggravation of their suffering.

A child with special needs is one who requires some form of special care due to physical, mental, emotional or health reasons. Children with special needs are also commonly referred to as children with disabilities. The Americans with Disabilities Act (ADA) defines a child with a disability more specifically as one who has a physical or mental impairment that substantially limits the child's ability to care for herself or himself, perform manual tasks, or engage in any other "major life activity," such as walking, seeing, hearing, speaking, breathing, or learning, in an age-appropriate manner.

The kind of disability a child might have can vary greatly allergies, moderate retardation, diabetes, cerebral palsy, or even a terminal illness may each be considered a disability under the ADA. A child with a disability can be one who is visually or hearing impaired, non-ambulatory, has a learning disability, or has an emotional or mental illness. Even a child with a severe behavioural problem, whom you or others might regard as having an emotional or mental disability, may be protected under the ADA, regardless of whether that child is, or can be, formally diagnosed as having a disability. Because each child is unique and has unique needs, no single approach to caring for children with disabilities can be applied to all children, or even to those with the same disability.

However, you should keep a few basic principles in mind. Children with disabilities are more similar than different from other children. Like all children, those with disabilities should be encouraged to help themselves as much as they can. You should know that:

- you can integrate many children with special needs into your present programme without changes in your routine or physical environment;
- some support services exist to help you care for children with special needs;
- and, best of all, the experience of working with children with special needs can be rewarding for everyone involved, children and adults alike.

Research indicates that the family reaction to the birth of a disabled child changes according to the type of disability and the child's diagnostic category. The differences are probably an indirect consequence of anticipated or actual reactions by those surrounding the disabled child and the family, in addition to parental reactions.

Many researchers have recently mentioned the positive coping and functioning of many families with developmentally disabled children. In the past there was a tendency to emphasize issues of illness and pressures, spousal strain and maladjustment within the family, while presently they are replaced with questions concerning positive adjustment, satisfaction, acceptance, and spousal harmony. Rather than perceiving the family as a helpless victim, it is perceived as a unit that adapts by a process of structuring.

Professionals must acknowledge the importance of the family and encourage them to have a positive attitude towards disability. They control decisions concerning the disabled child and the family.

When parents first learn that their child has a disability, they may experience feelings of grief. Parents often describe a sense of sadness and a feeling that the dreams they held for their child have been lost. Grief has many stages and may include a wide range of negative feelings. All of these feelings are perfectly valid. Allow yourself to mourn the loss of your original dreams, and know that acceptance and hope are sure to follow.

When parents learn that their child has a disability or a chronic illness, they begin a journey that takes them into a life that is often filled with strong emotion, difficult choices, interactions with many different professionals and specialists, and an ongoing need for information and services. Initially, parents may feel isolated and alone, and not know where to begin their search for information, assistance, understanding, and support.

Families are dynamic functioning units repeatedly propelled from situations of stability and balance to those of development and change. Individuals and their families evolve within a single system, constantly striving for balance. The birth of a child with developmental disabilities creates a severe breach of this balance and the family undergoes a difficult existential experience. Parents are the central and most important link in the care, education, and supervision of persons with intellectual disability (ID).

Despite this major role, the literature tends to minimize their significance. Even in Israel, despite the great importance of family, the role of parents is rarely discussed. Professional literature dealing with parents' patterns of coping with raising a handicapped/disabled child describes a wide spectrum of patterns, ranging from reactions of mourning and crisis to those of acceptance. It is very important to examine parents as coping people and the developmentally disabled as children, adolescents, and adults with special needs.

In such moments of realizing what is happening, you feel devastated, seem like your whole life is wrecked. On learning that their child may have a disability, most parents react in ways that have been shared by all parents before them who have also been faced with this disappointment and this enormous challenge.

Reactions for parents

One of the first reactions is **denial**— "This cannot be happening to me, to my child, to our family." Denial rapidly merges with anger, which may be directed toward the medical personnel who were involved in providing the information about the child's problem. In some parts of the world, they link it to happening around the family line and homeland where they come from more of an attack.

Anger can also colour communication between husband and wife or with grandparents or significant others in the family. Early on, it seems that the anger is so intense that it touches almost anyone, because it is triggered by the feelings of grief and inexplicable loss that one does not know how to explain or deal with.

Fear is another immediate response. People often fear the unknown more than they fear the known. Having the complete diagnosis and some knowledge of the child's future prospects can be easier than uncertainty. In either case, however, fear of the future is a common emotion: "What is going to happen to this child when he is five years old, when he is twelve, when he is twenty-one? What is going to happen to this child when I am gone?" Then other questions arise: "Will he ever learn? Will he ever go to college?

Will he or she have the capability of loving and living and laughing and doing all the things that we had planned? "Other unknowns also inspire fear.

Parents fear that the child's condition will be the very worst it possibly could be. Sometimes there is guilt over some slight committed years before toward a person with a disability.

There is also fear of society's rejection, fears about how brothers and sisters will be affected, questions as to whether there will be any more brothers or sisters in this family, and concerns about whether the husband or wife will love this child. These fears can almost immobilize some parents.

Then there is **guilt**—guilt and concern about whether the parents themselves have caused the problem: "Did I do something to cause this? Am I being punished for something I have done? Did I take care of myself when I was pregnant? Did my wife take good enough care of herself when she was pregnant?" Much self-reproach and remorse can stem from questioning the causes of the disability. Perhaps I was haunted by spirits which resulted in that?

Guilt feelings may also be manifested in spiritual and religious interpretations of blame and punishment. When they cry, "Why me?" or "Why my child?", many parents are also saying, "Why has God done this to me?" How often have we raised our eyes to heaven and asked: "What did I ever do to deserve this?" A young mother might think, "I feel so guilty because all my life I had never had a hardship and now God has decided to give me a hardship." Or Maybe my family line was cursed because of a wrong committed, and the curse now fell on me.

Confusion also marks this traumatic period. As a result of not fully understanding what is happening and what will happen, confusion reveals itself in sleeplessness, inability to make decisions, and mental overload. In the midst of such trauma, information can seem garbled and distorted.

You hear new words that you never heard before, terms that describe something that you cannot understand. You want to find out what it is all about, yet it seems that you cannot make sense of all the information you are receiving. Often parents are just not on the same wavelength as the person who is trying to communicate with them about their child's disability.

Powerlessness to change what is happening is very difficult to accept. You cannot change the fact that your child has a disability, yet parents want to feel competent and capable of handling their own life situations. It is extremely hard to be forced to rely on the judgments, opinions, and recommendations of others. Compounding the problem is that these others are often strangers with whom no bond of trust has yet been established.

Disappointment that a child is not perfect poses a threat to many parents' egos and a challenge to their value system. This jolt to previous expectations can create reluctance to accept one's child as a valuable, developing person.

Rejection is another reaction that parents experience. Rejection can be directed toward the child or toward the medical personnel or toward other family members. One of the more serious forms of rejection, and not that uncommon, is a "death wish" for the child— a feeling that many parents report at their deepest points of depression.

During this period of time when so many different feelings can flood the mind and heart, there is no way to measure how intensely a parent may experience this constellation of emotions. Not all parents go through these stages, but it is important for parents to identify with all of the potentially troublesome feelings that can arise, so that they will know that they are not alone. There are many constructive actions that you can take immediately, and there are many sources of help, communication, and reassurance.

What's the way out?

Rely on Positive Sources

In Your Life One positive source of strength and wisdom might be your minister, priest, or rabbi. Another maybe a good friend or a counsellor. Go to those who have been a strength before in your life. Find the new sources that you need now.

Do Not Be Intimidated

Many parents feel inadequate in the presence of people from the medical or educational professions because of their credentials and, sometimes, because of their professional manner. Do not be intimidated by the educational backgrounds of these and other personnel who may be involved in treating or helping your child. You do not have to apologize for wanting to know what is occurring.

Do not be concerned that you are being a bother or are asking too many questions.

Remember, this is your child, and the situation has a profound effect on your life and on your child's future. Therefore, itis important that you learn as much as you can about your situation.

Do Not Be Afraid to Show Emotion

So many parents, especially dads, repress their emotions because they believe it to be a sign of weakness to let people know how they are feeling. The strongest fathers of children with disabilities whom I know are not afraid to show their emotions. They understand that revealing feelings does not diminish one's strength.

Learn to Deal with Natural Feelings of Bitterness and Anger

Feelings of bitterness and anger are inevitable when you realize that you must revise the hopes and dreams you originally had for your child. It is very valuable to recognize your anger and to learn to let go of it. You may need outside help to do this. It may not feel like it, but life will get better and the day will come when you will feel positive again. By acknowledging and working through your negative feelings, you will be better equipped to meet new challenges, and bitterness and anger will no longer drain your energies and initiative.

Maintain a Positive Outlook

A positive attitude will be one of your genuinely valuable tools for dealing with problems. There is truly, always a positive side to whatever is occurring. Focusing on the positives diminishes the negatives and makes life easier to deal with.

Avoid Pity

Self-pity, the experience of pity from others, or pity for your child is actually disabling. Pity is not what is needed. Empathy, which is the ability to feel with another person, is the attitude to be encouraged.

Decide How to Deal with Others

During this period, you may feel saddened by or angry about the way people are reacting to you or your child. Many people's reactions to serious problems are caused by a lack of understanding, simply not knowing what to say, or fear of the unknown. Understand that many people don't know how to behave when they see a child with differences, and they may react inappropriately. Think about and decide how you want to deal with stares or questions. Try not to use too much energy being concerned about people who are not able to respond in ways you might prefer.

Remember That This is Your Child

This person is your child, first and foremost. Granted, your child's development may be different from that of other children, but this does not make your child less valuable, less human, less important, or in less need of your love and parenting. Love and enjoy your child. The child comes first; the disability comes second. If you can relax and take the positive steps just outlined, one at a time, you will do the best you can, your child will benefit, and you can look forward to the future with hope.

Parental reactions

The first type is called "the crisis of change" and it stems from the occurrence of an unexpected change in the individual's life and self-perception. This is not a reaction to the disability per se, rather to the sudden change in life circumstances. The second type of crisis is connected to the transformation of individual personal values as a result of the specific crisis. Most people have been educated according to an ethical system that stresses individual personal abilities and achievements. The birth of a disabled child requires parents to love a significant figure – their child, who is deprived of the ability to grant a feeling of achievement.

The result is bivalent feelings toward the child. A third type of crisis is called "the crisis of reality" and it stems from the harsh objective conditions formed by the need to raise a handicapped child: financial difficulties, limitation of the parents' free time, and the great deal of time that parents are required to devote to their child.

Two conflicting concepts may be discerned in the literature dealing with the effect of raising a developmentally disabled child on the family throughout its life cycle. One concept stresses burnout, stating that continuous burnout reduces family resources. The other focuses on the family's ability to adapt and states that in time the family adapts and acquires tools and experience which may help daily care and bestow renewed, positive meaning, on this reality.

However, positive manners of coping are not stressed in the professional literature, which tends to describe negative aspects of the coping process. The assumption is that the family's reaction to the handicapped child will change according to the type of disability. For example, the family will react differently to a visible disability than to a non-visible. *Kandel and Merrick: Children and Disability The Scientific World JOURNAL (2007) 7, 1799-1809* **disability** which is a hereditary developmental disability In the former case elements of self-blame are stressed. For example, families, according to the child's diagnostic category, report different levels of mourning and strain. It may be assumed that some of the diversity is an indirect outcome, not only of parental reactions but also, of anticipated or real environmental reactions to the disabled child and his family.

Following this idea, I assumed that the acceptance process of parents of physically disabled children would be easier than the acceptance process experienced by parents of children with (medium and lower) mental retardation i.e. parents of children with physical disabilities would report a normal level of family functioning, a better family atmosphere and a normal spousal relationship, compared to families of children with mental retardation.

The professional literature tends to minimize the parents, the family and their coping with the developmentally disabled child. The professional literature dealing with parents' coping patterns describes a range of patterns, from reactions of crisis and mourning to those of acceptance. Major emotions mentioned are guilt, denial, sorrow, tendency to over-protect and depression, and also patterns of parental acceptance.

While in the past research tended to focus on dysfunctional family coping and to assume that family reactions to the birth of a disabled child are mainly uniform, today there is more attention to successful family coping with crises.

The principle of normalization, the idea of integrating the disabled in the community, and even the developmental model, contributed to this transition in attitudes to family coping with the birth of a disabled child and to the development of an approach acknowledging a wide range of parental reactions.

Even if parents usually experience one or more of the crises discussed in the literature, including the crisis of change, the crisis of values, and the crisis of reality, most parents can adapt to reality and develop coping tools. Professional acknowledgement of these difficulties and family awareness of the normalcy of crisis reactions may help families currently in a state of imbalance.

You Are Your Child's Greatest Advocate

You know your child best. You will be well-suited to advocate on your child's behalf until he or she gets older and learns to be a self-advocate. Remember the goal of independence. Assume that people have your child's best interests in mind, but make sure they know what you think is in your child's best interest.

But after looking at all of these, then comes the question: who are they in God's Plan? Why did God decide to create them in such a manner? Most times, we really cannot tell and understand God's ways and how he handles life's situation.

But in the midst of all this chaos, you need to ask for his direction on what you have to do, how to cope and most importantly for His peace, you can't run from reality, but you can stay in it to ensure you bring out the best result and response needed.

I have not experienced it myself, but in other life situations I have faced, one thing usually comforts me, I am not the first to experience that and will not be the last, though it coincidentally happened to me as well, my response in that moment counts a lot.

Scripturally, Naaman was a disabled general in the Syrian Army who made and conducted military strategies for his master even though he was disable, he was a great man and the head of an army. The four disabled people in Israel brought about salvation from starvation to the whole nation and many other examples too tell us that there is ability in disability. Therefore, we should not give up when our child is physically disable.

At the moment, a disabled child can do things in almost every sector of life that a normal child can. they are in the sports, entertainment and other sectors you never expected you will see them fit in; be it the kind of condition, just know that your child is unique, has abilities that you can harness and make him become acceptable too.

A major problem of these kinds of ailments are with parents living in the remote areas of our countries, they need awareness and encouragement so as not to give in to the pressure that comes from the society and even within the family. Every child is a gift from God, first to the family and then to humanity, and at the appropriate time what God has destined for that child to become will surely suffice, you just stay put to encourage and bring out the best God has placed in your child. And someday, the rejected will become loved and celebrated. If Gods healing proves "impossible", His plans are always and indeed very possible in such cases, remember that.

Let me conclude with an experience I had which led to talking about the disabled child. Myself and other members of the Drama Unit of the Church accompanied a disabled NGO and School in the city of Jos called Open Door in a tour round some communities in the State. During the tour, all the team members who participated had a better understanding that these disabled children equally have a future as any normal child does, just that the pathway to destiny is different. It further enlightens us to realize that the parents of these innocent children are facing a lot and need to be encouraged and we were privileged to come with acting, and a lot of their fears were gone. But the greatest benefactors were us who acted, because it gave us a chance to know how important they equally are to the society irrespective of their present predicament.

The society and family must join hands in a collective effort to help in raising these innocent children to give them the same hope every child should have, and over time it will be an effort that is of worth.

Chapter 7

The Family and Development/ Relationship

What is Development?

It is the process of developing, or being developed; an event constituting a new stage in a changing situation; but Merriam Webster dictionary defines Development as the act or process of growing or causing something to grow or become larger or more advanced.

In my opinion, development is a stage/level that leads to a progression that is mental, physical, spiritual and so on.

Who is a Parent? Section 576 of the education act 1996 defines "Parent" as all natural parents whether they are married or not OR any person who, although not a natural parent, has parental responsibility for a child or young person.

What is Parental Responsibility? Having parental responsibility means assuming all the rights, duties, responsibilities and authority that a parent of a child has by law.

People other than a child's natural parents can acquire responsibility through:

- Being granted a residence order
- Being appointed a guardian
- Being named in an emergency protection order

Child Discipline

What is Discipline? According to the Oxford Advanced Learners Dictionary, Discipline is "a practice of training people to obey rules and orders and punishing them if they do not; the controlled behaviour or situation that results from this training" OR "The ability to control your behaviour or the way you live, work etc. OR "to punish somebody for something they have done". Also, the Bible sees discipline according to the Greek word *sophronismos* meaning sober OR *Paideia* meaning "instruction", OR Hebrew *mucar* meaning "chastisement". In my opinion, discipline is then an instruction given to a child not with the aim of making him bad, but making him/her good so that when he/she grows in that manner of discipline will birth what the disciplinarian has proposed.

Discipline is an aspect of the 21st Century Church and society which had actually started from the inception of creation, but most Christian homes and communities at large are really lacking or ignoring it. And then as a result of that, the upcoming generation becomes a victim of what they never proposed or planned. When a child is growing he is entitled to learn as many things as possible under discipline and in whatever way possible. He has no option than to learn whatever comes by, now it might not be only through words, action or written, but can be either written or verbal. So, when you see a child of this present time, respect for older ones has ceased to exist, he/she talks without control, rarely says sorry when wrong, always has this sense of thinking "always right" etc. I always recall telling my mother, if I get married and bear my own children I will not allow them to come to her alone, rather we will come together and then leave again. Why? While we were growing, we knew our mummy to be stricter to our father so that while punishing us, whatever she lays her hand on becomes an instrument of punishment or discipline. So, whenever we are wrong, we always know of her next step, so either we stand a far distance with the preparation to speed off once she bends or go inside, because we know that when she comes out, she will also speed off trying to grab you. Worst of it is when she grabs you and traps you under her two legs, then neither our father nor anyone can come to your rescue; so we grew up with this level of training that you have to be careful not to do what will attract punishment from mummy, but all of a sudden as age caught up with her, she now changed from being a disciplined mother to a protective one. So that when you try to discipline in a subtle way to the one she used to administer it becomes a crime. But that is by the way, discipline sets you on a path to know the difference between what is good from what is bad, so that as you live, walk and interact with others in your day to day living, you walk with that mentality.

So now, when you see a child who comes from a wealthy family and the other who comes from a middle class family and also the other who also comes from a poor family, you tend to see the variation in discipline and behaviour. But discipline in itself has no boundary, you can see the child of a wealthy man not disciplined and that of a poor person more disciplined, because the way both of them were trained were also different. So discipline is a process that a child needs to grow in, and it does not refer to the physical only, but also to the mind, speech, reaction to situations, manner of approach, thinking capacity, way of life and living with people of different culture, background and lifestyle. Now if a father or mother possesses this quality, then a child also grows to imitate that same process, making discipline to be like the passing of a baton from one generation to another. On daily basis, I interact with people of my age and then I realize that almost all that have been well disciplined are having that burden in heart, of why the discipline they got has been bridged, so it's always more like it will never happen in my own time when I get married, so that always makes me ask these questions: What happened to the discipline we got while growing up? What makes it different from the discipline we are not seeing and facing reality?

The Bible says in Proverbs 23:13-14, [13]Do not withhold correction from a child, for if you beat him with a rod, he will not die; [14] you shall beat him or her with a rod and deliver his soul from hell (NKJV);

Withhold not discipline from the child; for if you strike *and* punish him with the [reed like] rod, he will not die. [14]You shall whip him with the rod and deliver his life from Sheol. (AMP);

[13]Always correct children when they need it. If you spank them, it will not kill them. [14]In fact, you might save their lives. Easy-to-Read Version

Now from my own understanding, there are two basic kinds of discipline, the physical and the inner discipline.

Physical Discipline

If a small child tries to touch an electric cable or fire or anything harmful, the parent hits the child's hand, why? So that the child will know that it is either dangerous or showing him/he that it is bad. So, at times when the child goes near he/she will be careful not to touch it because of the fear of been beating/spanked, but if the child is allowed the privilege to touch it and is burnt or harmed by that substance or thing, he/she learns by experience that that thing was harmful, and then disciplines himself/herself not to go through that path again; if a child wears a cloth that exposes either his/her body parts and was scolded at and asked to go and change, then the child knows and learns that, that manner of dressing is wrong; if a child shouts at or disobeys an elder and is spanked, then he/she knows that it is wrong to shout at or disobey an elder; if a child refuses to say sorry and is been spanked then the child learns that refusing to say sorry is wrong; if a child fights and is beaten or spanked, the child knows that fighting is bad; in general, anything that physically contrast discipline and the child is beaten or spanked for that, the child learns from that and then begins to build a positive character and habit round those physical discipline process learned while growing, even unto adulthood and old age. One more thing to say is that, as the child grows in age, understanding, wisdom, and maturity, then he also sees those childhood spanking has been baseless/useless because he/she is now being faced with higher issues that will not cause spanking physically but will allow him/her to apply maturity, wisdom and understanding. So, Proverbs 22:6 talks about this pattern of discipline.

Inner (Oral or Verbal) Discipline.

At this level or stage, the child should have reached a certain age of reasoning, knowing the difference between right and wrong, good and bad, and then physical discipline now becomes irrelevant. So what needs to be applied in this stage is the discipline of the mind; the Bible says that when David was dying, he called his son Solomon after declaring him king (1 Kings 2:1-5) and gave him counsel on how to handle kingship and his people in Israel and also how to give wise counsel and judgment. Had it been he was given these procedures as a child, he would not have understood the value of what his father meant, but the father allowed him to reach and attain the position of kingship first. Now as the child grows, as a parent you begin to engage him in house chores to know that marriage is a joint process where the husband must assist the wife not only financially but through little house chores too; a child wakes up in the morning for devotion and then the father's there either in prayers or sharing the word of God too; parents sit with their children and laugh as well play and interact on the level of a family; child sees parents hugging, playing with each other and then advising each other; watch them sharing experience of how they were nearly involved in a shabby deal at place of work; mummy sharing an experience with her boss. Now these are established facts of discipline the child grows with in mind: Love, faithfulness, care, trust, truth, openness, now these are now disciplines taught to the child physically, but he/she grows to see them and then learns to discipline himself/herself in that manner as he/she has seen in the family. This type of discipline speaks for itself through the quality of its practice in the home; at times you have to say it to them and at times you have to let the child learn without resentment (unless on the basis of questions asked).

On the other hand, verbal discipline can go through advice too, a child really needs to learn in almost all ramifications of life. And though teachers, religious leaders and other people play important roles in that, the parent and family plays a more important role in shaping the child. A child comes back from school with an unsatisfactory result, you are not expected to shout at him/her, they need encouraging words that will boost their morale for the next upcoming school term/session. While I was teaching in the primary school I was privileged to interact with those from the secondary school as well, so one of the students did not have a good result as she was thinking or expecting, so she looked worried and down casted, so when I saw her I asked her what was wrong and she told me that her result was not good enough. Then I told her that that it is not something to be worried about, all she has to do is brace up and fight back in the next coming term, never relent in her reading and always dedicate a special time to read and study hard Though I was not there the next term they resumed, but the next term when I went for a visit, instead of a worrying face I saw a smiling face, and I asked her as usual how far? And all she could say was there was serious improvement, and since then she has improved her grades and performance; now this is a teacher and student, so if she comes home and the same words were said to her then it now lets herknow she has to work hard.

Words are very powerful in the life and development of a child, so parents should never open their mouth to say to their children "you cannot make it", "you dumb head", or any foul or abusive words that will demoralize the spirit of that child, either big or small. I remembered a father once speaking had said his child offended him badly, and he opened his mouth to abuse the child. But all that came out of his mouth was "God bless you" and then both of them laughed, and that settled the case. A child can always think he/she is right, but it is your duty to sit him/her down and advise him/her to know that they are not always right, and even if they are right then at times it is good to admit the defensive part to let peace prevail. So if a child steals as an adult, then you sit him down and talk to him, making him/her know that at his/her age they should begin to start planning on starting their own home and not steal or indulge in any act that can ruin their reputation. At times you just need to tell them one word, build a reputation and integrity that will last and take your name beyond the shores you have ever imagined or think of, but be careful not to also destroy what you have built, because it can take you years to build that and then within a twinkling of an eye you have destroyed everything. A child who is ready to listen will do that and then put it into action, and another will listen but not apply immediately, while another will play with such advice. But know that as a parent, you must administer your own part in that, so that "he who has an ear will hear and save his soul from death", just like this popular saying "you can force a horse to the river, but cannot force it to drink from it", so also is a child. So when you do your own part, then you need to let God now do His own part in the development of the child.

Parents, you need to know that a quality foundation set for your family enhances not only the development of your child and family but also that of the society and church. So the type of disciplinarian you are now, defines the type of children that will get to graduate from your school of discipline.

So how can this kind of discipline be administered? Such discipline has one method: the Bible and others.

Relationship

Relationship is also a very key aspect in the development of a child. It's one aspect that can be described as a fragile thing, once it breaks it becomes difficult to bring it back to its real shape again. Definitions say Relationship "is the way in which two or more people or things are connected or state of being connected". It also varies, between friends, countries, two lovers, groups, people, family member's etc. But what we will be looking at here is the relationship that exists within the family as a unit of the society. So, we can define a relationship in this context as a bond that connects a father, mother, child/children together, leading to trust, love, openness, intimacy and protection. On this ground, we will be considering a series of relationships within this unit, its effectiveness and benefit.

It is also an agreement or an understanding between two parties of equal level or of a higher level to the lower. The essence of a relationship is so that the parties can have a better understanding and love, and can cherish each other while having equal rights.

Parents-child relationship

If a child is not able to depend on his/her earthly parents during challenges and troubles faced at their ages of growth then the family is out for a risk that will be difficult to control; and when a child begins to feel comfortable in being with friends, gadgets and anything that can keep him/her company rather than having interactions with his parents then there arises a need for a serious check on that. And if you as father or mother cannot spare some time to have meaningful interactive sessions with your child about life, studies, challenges and talks about current issues, and other things that will give them a chance to open and express themselves openly to you and understand you, then this should serve as a call up for you to begin that now. Because a father, mother and children are meant to be the best friends ever, so that when the child learns to open up about several issues with you then even when the child does the wrong thing, he/she knows what you are capable of doing at such moments. Now you need to also know that this is the basis of it all, you don't develop it when the child has come of age, you develop it from childhood to adulthood. Looking at Jesus and His earthly parents there is this cordial relationship that existed, so that they not only knew the kind of child they had but also knew how to treat Him and allow Him express Himself over certain issues. Another good example of this kind of relationship is that of Job, his wife and the children. The Bible tells us that whenever the children finish their own celebration and offer their sacrifices together, he will also offer sacrifices on their behalf "maybe they have sinned and cursed God in their hearts", Job 1:4&5. This kind of attitude and character shows that there is a level of understanding and communication that binds this family together to the extent that the parents will do that kind of habit to their children. So, can that habit or lifestyle still exist? Do we have parents who have developed this level of relationship with their children that the children can share issues with their parents without telling others? The answer is all yes, but what it implies here is that if your family is not experiencing such a relationship then you can make a decision to see it work too. At times you see a child closer to the mother or the father, all these are mediums that can be used to develop this kind of relationship.

"Children's physical and emotional statuses, as well as their social and cognitive development, greatly depend on their family dynamics. The rising incidence of behavioural problems among children could suggest that some families are struggling to cope with the increasing stresses they are experiencing.

Family dynamics

Many characteristics of families have changed during a period of three to five decades.

- In England and Wales, 53% of children were born within marriage in 2013, compared to 59% in 2003 and 93% in 1963.

- The average age of marriage has increased and more children are born to women older than 30 years.

- In the UK, there were 2.0 million lone parents with dependent children in 2015. This figure has grown steadily from 1.9 million in 2005. Lone parents with dependent children represented 25% of all families with dependent children in 2015 - a similar level to 2005.

- It is estimated that the proportion of marriages ending in divorce is 42%. Nearly half (48%) of couples divorcing in 2013 had at least one child aged under 16 living in the family.

- The percentage of women working has increased and there has been an increase in paternal involvement in childcare".

"One face of the parent-child relationship resembles that of the teacher-student relationship.

Psychologists call the relationship between child and parent "attachment." Attachment theory, or the study of these relationships, has shed light on the importance of the relationships between parent and child as well as pointed out some of the key steps parents can take to raise their children well. In addition, mothers and fathers take on different roles in bringing up a well-developed child." (*Damon Verial*)

Warmth in Parent-child Relationships

The warmth that parents bring to their children's lives starts at infancy. Moms and dads of young children shower their kids with baby-talk and physical touch. These behaviours show the child that others are sensitive to their needs and that parents can be relied on for emotional responsiveness. As a child grows older, he finds warmth in the parent-child relationship in other ways, specifically in receiving the fulfilment of his emotional needs, whether they be play or intimate conversation. Warmth in parenting can lead to a cooperative child, who is well-developed socially and emotionally.

Promoting Independence

As ironic as it may sound, it is parents who are to take the lead in teaching their children not to rely on their parents. Indeed, much of being a parent is teaching a child to do things for herself, from using the toilet to driving a car. One important part of this aspect of the parent-child relationship is disciplining children, which often is a way of keeping children on track in their own initiatives. Setting limits, such as restricting the amount of television time per day, helps children stay focused on their own responsibilities, such as finishing homework. Without parents, the phase of growing up in childhood would decrease in speed.

Teaching

From early childhood, the home becomes a school. To parents of older children, this is obvious, as after dinner the dinner table might become the family study table. However, parents' roles in educating young children start as early as the toddler years.

Parents simultaneously educate their children while they strengthen the parent-child attachment. For example, reading books to your child will strengthen her linguistic development, playing active games with your child will improve her motor-skill development and finishing puzzles with your child will enhance her cognitive development. Young children -- and even parents -- might mistakenly believe they are just spending quality time with family when they are actually developing useful life skills. (*Damon Verial*)

The Importance of Mom and Dad

A mother and father play different roles in the development of a child. The differences can be roughly summed up in the following way: Moms are protectors and educators; dads are life coaches and counselors. Moms act as a safe foundation on which children can rely; they teach their children not to be afraid of new surroundings. Moreover, as moms tend to spend more time engaging in low-intensity activities, such as reading and game-playing with their children, children begin to see mothers as teachers.

The father's role in a child's development has traditionally been underestimated. According to researchers Ross Parke and Kevin MacDonald, and authors of the article "Parent-Child Physical Play," which appeared in the journal Sex Roles, fathers play an integral role in the emotional and social development of children. Father-child interaction tends to be more intense, and through their shared activities children learn how to express and control their emotions with their fathers. By working together, mothers and fathers help their children develop their skills across the spectrum. (*Damon Verial*)

Father-child relationship

There is this popular saying "like father like son, like mother like daughter". In some cases, it's even the daughter that is more close to the father compared to the male child. The father is the head of the house, so belongs to every member of the house with no differences shown. And any father that has his child as his friend should count that as a big privilege; I was talking to a series of children and was asking whom they loved most, and just a few hands were raised to support their fathers, and when I asked why? Most said that father beats, some said he shouts and many other testimonies. So even if with this kind of lifestyle you still have your children running to you, then it means you are really a father, but maybe it still implies that you need to change the method or manner of approach with the child. If I might give you a little example, a child after being wrong and accepting he/she is wrong, needs a little show of love and then correction to understand where he was wrong and then next time I believe the same thing will not be done again. Fathers, though the Bible says love your wives and then children should obey their parents, but permit me to add that, as a father you need to draw your child closer to you than anyone else. Let them know how much you love, care, provide and are always ready to listen to them and moreover also give them your attention. When we look at the relationship between Joseph and his father also, David and his father, and many more examples, we will get to know that just as the love of a mother has no boundary so should be that of the father.

Mother-child relationship

If in the family the child cannot be close to either the mother or father, then it's a serious disaster which can really affect the total development of the child from childhood to adulthood. It is believed that mothers are the carriers of virtually all the burden in the family: training, cooking, household maintenance, and to an extent building of the family relationship etc. So if as the mother, you don't have the habit of character that welcomes visitors and people from the side of your husband, then definitely it automatically shows that that is the same way you behave towards your children/child. Because it has been an established fact that the same way you treat your own, should be the same way you treat others.

If a mother is open to her children/child, then the possibility of her virtually influencing every decision and choices they make is paramount. The wife to my uncle tends to be one of the closest people I have known in my life, so there are issues that I can share with her that I might not be able to open up about to my wife; but her children are a little bit afraid of her, why? They see their mother as being fierce and too strict. So several times, most especially for the last daughter, she prefers the company of her father to the mother. Looking at the Bible and the relationship of Jesus with His earthly mother, it shows he is more close to His mother than the father, and that is seen during the miracle of turning of water into wine, John 2:1-7, so that when she told Him to do that she just told them to do as He had said, because she believed that her son will do what she said. That's the level of intimacy and influence she had over her son; so if as a mother your child cannot obey some level of instructions you give, then there is a gap that has been created for a long time or a gap has begun to be created and will make it impossible for your child to adhere to the basic instructions you give them. Mothers, I therefore urge you to know and begin to work with the realization of one thing: that children can be free with their fathers but most of their lives, and almost throughout their development stages, should have some great level of influence championed by you. Being strict and firm is not bad, shouting and beating is not bad as well and all other things administered, but all must be done in love.

Another aspect I will love to talk about is prayer, mothers work hard as well as fathers. I grew up in a family where I knew that my grand dad is the one who takes his time every night to pray for his children, grandchildren and other issues, but my mother also caught the light and has been the one who use to pray. And then when you look at almost all through history of people who did great exploits, they always give the credit to the prayers of their mothers as what helped them all through their developmental stages; so if you are a mother or an intended mother in the future you need to know that the large chunk of the development of your husband, children and family lies in your hands. A child can sometimes neglect his/her father because of some issues, but a child can never neglect the mother for many reasons; so you either take your place now in the development of your child or the whole pressure and burden as well as worries now lies on you.

Also, most kings in the Bible have more links to the mother than the father, because the father always goes for wars and only has time to deal with issues within his kingdom and other kingdoms, so most of the time the mother is the one that trains and disciplines the child so that whatever the child later grows up to become is as a result of that which he/she has heard and learned from their mother. So if as a mother, you take your relationship with your child/children casually that's how they will also take your influence over their affairs casually, and as well if you take it serious they will also take your influences serious; but do not also use that avenue of the influence you have over them to teach them negative behaviour and lifestyle that rather than build them and set them on the rock and also path of success will rather end up corrupting their lives and causing them to abuse privileges they should have taken dare to heart; so mothers, with more emphasis the influence you have over your child can either make him/her or destroy him/her as well, all you need to do is take the right decision and use the opportunity you have now to enhance and positively initiate the development of your child's life through the relationship you have developed over time.

Child-child relationship

Permit me to say that, in the present dispensation we are in now, this is the latest trend of the 21st century. Going back a little to the Bible, King Rehoboam, the son of Solomon who led to the division of the kingdom (1 Kings 12) is a very powerful example of this scenario. But if I may ask, is it the fault of a child to build trust with a fellow brother, sister and friend? The answer is no, reason being that what a child cannot get or benefit from his father or mother, he/she believes that there is the high possibility of getting it from his friends or peers. So you see a child running away or not always staying at home but spending more time with friends, is always a result of what is not gotten from home. Friendship is not bad, but reaching a point that a child is literally distant from his/her parents and then prefers staying longer with friends is not the best. Because in such moments, the child is then faced with a lot of pressure, pressure to adapt and fill the gap lost in the family or pressure to change from a negative attitude to a positive one.

Back in the biblical times, David and Jonathan (1 Kings 18) were very good friends to the extent that Jonathan whose father was the present King was not scared of forfeiting his father's throne for his best friend, but then looking at the company also kept by Rehoboam, you definitely will know that that company is a type of company that will not just ruin relationship but even reputation. So the company a child keeps is very important to him/her and also to you as parents.

The 21st century child believes that he/she has lost a lot and a wide gap has been created between the child and the parent, so he/she prefers to stay close to his gadget and a friend or friends most of the time. Child to child relationship is very important though, in the development of a child, but is also risky if the child finds himself/herself in the company of people who don't have the ability to think positively and as well lay a solid foundation that will aid them in life.

I watched a movie about three friends who met in a tertiary institution in India. Though from different backgrounds, but they got to love each other and were also studying engineering, so that they either are in one trouble together or moving out of another together; but the mystery/tragedy is that one of them always comes first while the other two are always second to the last and last respectively, reason being that one is afraid so always wears rings and then performs incantations as a way of gaining favour from the gods in other to pass his exams, while the other faces due pressure from his parents and in order to please them decides to also study engineering while his real calling and passion was photography. And the last one really had a passion to study and was virtually good at science and technology was actually pretending to be someone else and studying in his place. So the other two out of fear never made it as it were to be, until they came into each other's company and then as they grew and built the relationship, he was able to change their mental status as well as most part of their lives positively and then help them grow to achieve their individual dreams and purpose.

The relationship of this present stage is based on: reducing peer pressure, running from responsibilities in the house, afraid of being shouted at etc. But if it were possible for them to see beyond just some of these reasons, to understand and then place higher priorities on our friendship/relationship to others, that will do a lot good to them

Older and Younger Ones Relationship

The totality of a child's growth and development solely depends on the state in which the parents are…considering the story of Esau and Jacob in this context; the mother loved Jacob and will not compromise that love while the father loved Esau because he was the first child, and that order cannot be compromised, because of the prophecy that accompanied his coming "Gen. 25:23- The Lord said to her, The Founders of two nations are in your womb, and the separation has begun in your body; the one people shall be stronger than the other, and the elder shall serve the younger (AMP)"; so at all cost she had to ensure it comes to pass.

Even though in the long run, the prophecy still came to pass; but a rift has been created between the two children by the parents; the position of a parent in maintaining and strengthening the relationship between the older and younger ones depends on the outcome in the near future; you cannot love one child against another, be it all boys or girls and expect them to learn to be united and love one another in your absence... A parent must build the future he/she wants for his/her children while he/she is still living so that in absence they know that there won't be space for compromise...be it in the sharing of inheritance or any other activity that they feel is of importance. Parents must as well insist on the place of order in terms of positioning in the family; this really helps to maintain order and respect within the circle of the children.

Even though the African parent is doing his/her best in restoring that order, some families still have children which they prefer to others, and all the children notice that; the others might not say a word, but a day will come that it cannot be hidden. Pray that it happens while you are watching so you can amend the mistakes; because when it does happen when you are no more, then you cannot imagine the damage it can lead to. An example of this is the story of Joseph; even though thiswas a prophecy, a gap was created in the lives of the 12 children of Jacob...it took time for the gap to be covered but the damage had been done.

Parents, you play a vital role in what kind of relationship your children build at the family level; because that will be noticed in their day to day activities in your absence.

Now, an older brother/sister must understand that his/her position in the family is to ensure that a good example is shown to the other children; when you as the older child is responsible, it becomes difficult for those behind you to be irresponsible; unless you don't really show them how to live a life that is worth emulating. You serve as the father and mother in their absence, and I believe at that level you can learn to tame every anti-godly thought that rises from your other siblings; because one of your major responsibility is becoming the light they will glean on to see clearly; but that also depends on your spiritual standing and understanding too. So if you cannot fill in the void of the light to them, then you might equally have to take blame for them not living right; also, we must learn to abuse that thought that am I my brother/sister's keeper? If you are not, then God will not place you in that position, he entrusted you to be able to handle the position of the first child...so you as the first child are responsible for whatever your younger siblings become.

It can't be denied that most times, the younger ones too have their own faults and shortcomings; but that will solely depend on whether the older one takes his/her responsibility or not. In African culture, it is better a male to be the first child than a female; because he commands respect to her and can easily tame whatever negative behaviour that is proceeding from his younger ones to her. If you are a younger child, have the attitude of Joseph, have that of David, have that of Solomon amongst others; when you humble and submit yourselves to your older ones, I so much believe that instead of having issues they will always protect you, and ensure that your interests and worries are theirs. God placed them in that position on purpose, in the absence of our parents they fill the void; and always remember that no matter how high you have gone or will go in life, they have been placed before you, so you must respect and submit to them...Just as you will need the blessings of your parents, you will equally need theirs.

Abuse of relationship

As stated above, many times if some things are done in excess; it becomes a very serious issue. Abuse can come from the side of the child or from the adult; if it comes from the children we can easily say it's as a result of being a child or not understanding, but what if it comes directly from the older one? Then it becomes dangerous and at times unbearable. On this note, we will look at abuse from the child's perspective.

Human Trafficking

Though our area of interest is on child trafficking, we will take a while to have a general look at what trafficking is.

Human trafficking is modern day slavery! It is when people are forced, kidnapped or deceived to work as labourers or prostitutes against their will, and without pay. It is the exploitation of some people by some other people. For example; when some people unfairly use other people for personal gain. These people are either taken from one location to another, both locally and internationally or, even within their homes and neighbourhoods.

Human trafficking is a crime that is hidden, because people do not know what it is or how it happens, so they cannot identify it when they see it happening. Increasingly, criminal organizations such as gangs, etc. are luring children from schools into commercial sexual exploitation or trafficking.

Every year, millions of men, women, and children are trafficked in countries around the world –including Nigeria. Many of these victims are deceived with false promises of money or a better life; instead, they are forced, coerced or deceived into commercial sex, domestic servitude, or other types of forced labour.

Any child under the age of 18 who is forced to have sex with anyone is a victim of human trafficking according to human trafficking law, regardless of whether there is force, fraud, or coercion.

Facts about Human Trafficking:

1. Globally, the average cost of a slave is N14, 130.

2. Trafficking primarily involves exploitation which comes in many forms, including:

o Forcing victims into prostitution
o Subjecting victims to slavery or involuntary servitude
o Compelling victims to commit sex acts for the purpose of creating pornography
o Misleading victims into debt bondage

3. There are approximately 20-30 million slaves in the world today.

4. According to the U.S. State Department, 600,000 to 800,000 people are trafficked across international borders every year. More than 70 percent are female and half are children.

5. The International Labour Organization (ILO) estimates that 1.2 million children are trafficked each/every year.

6. International Labour Organization (ILO) estimates that there are as many as 1.8 million children sexually trafficked worldwide. UNICEF estimates as many as 2 million.

7. Girls are at a higher risk of being trafficked because of inequality.

8. There is no specific estimate/number of how many children are trafficked yearly because of the criminal and covert nature of the practice/crime; it is a hidden crime. However, in Africa according to ILO, estimates of 200,000 children are being trafficked yearly. Child trafficking is most prevalent in developing countries and Nigeria is one.

9. The major international instrument used in dealing with trafficking of children is titled **Protocol To Prevent**, which suppresses and punishes trafficking in persons, especially women and children and is part of the 2006 United Nations Palermo Protocols. The trafficking of children often involves both labour and migration and international frameworks clarify that these practices are illegal.

Who is Involved in Human Trafficking?

Human traffickers can be men or women, boys or girls, citizens of your country Nigeria, your state and even your neighbourhood, and they could also be foreigners i.e. people from another country. Human trafficking can involve school age youth, particularly those made vulnerable by unstable family situations, or who have little or no social support. The children at risk are not just primary/secondary school students, children of various ages are trafficked into sex slavery or forced labour.

Human traffickers may target young people through social media like; Facebook, twitter, whatsapp, websites, telephone chats, after school programmes, on the streets, in the market or shops, or through other students and friends who are used by traffickers to recruit victims. In fact, a person can be trafficked without ever leaving his/her hometown, state or village as the case may be.

We will introduce human trafficking as child trafficking as we are dealing with young people. Thus, child trafficking can take a variety of forms including sex slavery or prostitution, or forced labour. Those who are involved in trafficking children for sexual reasons or any other reasons are breaking the law, even if there is no force, fraud or coercion. Traffickers often look out for young people hoping for a better life, lacking parental/guardian care, having unstable family life, or with a history of sexual abuse condition amongst others.

***Note that human trafficking/child trafficking victims are found in cities, towns, and rural areas of your country and other countries as well.**

Reasons Why Child Trafficking Exists

These among others are possible reasons why human trafficking exists:

- **Money-** When a person is willing to give out another person to another person for sexual gratification or forced labour because he or she wants money from this exchange. Selfish gain makes people traffic others.

- **Ignorance-**When the community is unaware of this issue/vice, and when the government and community institutions are not trained to respond and report human trafficking.

- **Legislation-** When there are ineffective or dormant laws to address the crime of human trafficking, when there is no safety for victims who we know exist and when law enforcement does not investigate and punish people caught in human trafficking.

- **Laziness-** People don't want to work to earn money; rather they want the fastest means to getting money. However, a fast means of making money is wrong. The idea of making money through this criminal business is thrilling to people. Why? Because, evil is in the heart of men. People do anything to get money, even sell their fellow humans, brothers, sisters, daughters, sons, etc.

- Human trafficking exists because people are in need of cheap labour to their own advantage and they are also willing to pay for commercial sex.

Why do you Need to Know?

- Because everyone, especially young girls and boys like you are vulnerable to being trafficked. And, nowadays, traffickers prefer young girls and even young boys, because most of their clients want the trafficked victims for sex trafficking, and they make more money out of that. So, they are out for young people like you, and they go to any extent to get you.

- Awareness of the crime of child trafficking is the first step to eradicating this modern day slavery. We have to be able to recognize and identify the signs of human trafficking, report and support those who are actively fighting against human trafficking and punish the traffickers. Child trafficking can only be eradicated by an informed public, therefore you and I need to know about it so as to help fight against this evil.

The objective of child trafficking is often child exploitation, specifically to children under a predetermined minimum age, usually 14 years at the lowest. However, it goes as low as 5 years in Nigeria. Child trafficking takes different forms, however, the major trends that are predominant in Nigeria are:

a) **Forced Child Labour-** Forced labour is when a child is overworked against his/her will, agreement or acceptance. Usually children as young as 5 years old can become victims.

   Note that there is nothing wrong when children are engaged in light work as it is a form of home training that is morally and culturally accepted in our society. However, any child who is forced, or coerced into involuntary servitude, is a victim of human trafficking regardless of location. Child labour has many forms. These include:

   1. **Domestic servitude**: a person who does house work

   2. **Drug trades**

   3. **Agricultural Labourers**: A person who works in farms/plantations

   4. **Children Soldiers**

Child begging- Child begging is a type of begging in which boys and girls under the age of 16 are tricked into begging for money or food on the streets and neighbourhoods through psychological or physical coercion.

a) **Sexual Exploitation-** use of boys and girls in sexual activity whether in cash or kind. It is also child prostitution on the streets or indoors e.g. brothels, beer parlours, hotels, neighbourhood, schools, restaurants etc. Using boys and girls for the promotion and distribution of pornography and indecent adverts. When children are used in sex shows or strip clubs either privately or publicly. One major form of Sexual exploitation is **Forced Prostitution**, where young people are taken from one place to the other in order for them to have sex with other people against their will for money/personal gain. Sexual exploitation or sex trafficking, as the case maybe, can occur because of debt bondage, as young girls and even women are forced to continue in prostitution through the use of unlawful 'debt' incurred through their transportation or recruitment or their crude sale which so called 'madams' insist they must pay off before they can be free.

b) **Baby Factory** is a place where women willingly or unwillingly are forced to get pregnant and give up their babies for sale.

Reasons that could be why baby factories exist:

1. **Rituals-** Some people believe that using babies for rituals brings luck, success or favour, money, wealth, etc.

2. **Adoption-** Some of the babies from baby factories are sold for adoption or given for fostering to barren women, or couples who need to raise children not biologically theirs due to medical reasons, or other best known to them.

3. **Childlessness- To** buttress on the given point above, in cases where couples are unable to deliver due to reasons of unproductivity, they opt in for the option of going to such places to get one and raise a child.

4. **Child Pornography- This** is when children are depicted in images or pictures performing sexual acts with other children, adults and objects. People make billions of dollars from this through photographs, books, audiotapes, video etc.

5. The children are subjected to exploitation, rape, and paedophilia and in worse cases, murder. Pornography is usually an entrance into sex slavery/trafficking. Many traffickers force or deceive children into pornography as a way of conditioning them into believing that what they are doing is acceptable i.e. they make them believe that it is right. These traffickers may then use this pornography to get money from other people.

6. **Forced Marriage- This** is when a young girl is forced to marry against her will. **Forced marriage** is different from **Arranged Marriage**, because **Arranged Marriage** is when families plan for their children with the hope that the children would meet and have a relationship that would lead to marriage. In **Arranged Marriage**, both boy and girl would have to like and agree to marry each other, while in **Forced Marriage**, the young girl is coerced or threatened into marrying someone against her will and she may suffer violence if she refuses the marriage or sometimes the girl could be murdered by the family member or close friend, etc.

Effects Of Child Trafficking

1. Death or permanent injury of the victims trafficked because of the stage of trafficking or exploitation, such as hazardous working conditions, denied access to health care, domestic violence, beating, victims being starved to ensure obedience, drugged as payment or to cause addiction so they become dependent on the trafficker.

2. Depression: Due to some negative experiences either from home or life circumstances, some children go into depression and might need a change of environment in order to lay off these thoughts, unfortunately they sometimes end up becoming victims.

3. Families never get to see their children.

4. This act brings shame to the families especially if the victims who are sexually exploited are girls. So even

when they escape and return home, they are often rejected and in some cases disowned.

5. Corruption in the society- this could happen especially when many children are often trafficked from the same community, social development is hindered as trafficked children's education is cut short, they most times do not end up becoming useful or productive because of the lack of education.

6. Most of the victims face marital challenges because nobody wants to marry someone that was once a prostitute.

7. The nation's economy and development is severely hindered because of the lack of education of trafficked children, as children are the future of every nation.

Prevention:

There are 3 major levels to stop human trafficking from happening. These include:

1: Before

2: During

3: After

Before; this is before the act of human trafficking happens. There are things one needs to know that would prepare one to fight human trafficking:

Use body language when responding to strangers on the streets: For example - when saying NO, shake your head vehemently, so your NO is emphasized.

Run-away when or if your response is not working.

Shout to alert people around if the trafficker tries to forcefully grab you.

Be firm, bold and confident when responding.

Do not make friends with girls and boys that are stubborn, love boys/girls, and are always talking about making quick money, because they are likely the ones that can easily trick you into making quick money.

Before you agree to go anywhere with your friends you must inform your parents, siblings, guardian or an adult in your neighbourhood about where you are going and when you would be back.

Never just agree to follow your friend without knowing where. Also you must know in detail, where you are going. Do not be quick to go on outings to strange or new places by yourself.

You must pray. Prayer is very important. If you pray, God will answer and tell you whether to follow or not and which place to go and not to go. Being a child of God gives you a better chance of not being trafficked. How? Because God's protection is around you, and as you pray God uses diverse ways that we don't even know to protect us.

However, you must take heed to all you have learnt today, so as not to fall into the hands of traffickers.

Be wise. If it sounds too good to be true, it is probably not true. Plan to work hard to make money, do not expect someone to come and give you money for nothing. Chasing empty dreams gets a lot of girls in trouble.

During: this is simply avoiding human trafficking when you find yourself with a trafficker. These are what to do: **Scream-Hit-Run-Report.**

Children traffickers can be people known to families of the victim, but they come in disguise because of the motive they have. In cases where the child notices the strange action of such person around him/her, there is a need to quickly take action by screaming in terms of advances made, try to break free from the trafficker's grip when held, run to avoid being a victim and any danger unseen, then report to authorities so that immediate action can be taken to avoid other innocent children from been victims.

After: What next, if someone becomes a victim? There two basic steps to take:

A.   Forgive yourself, and then forgive the traffickers.

Be willing to step out. This simply means to seek counseling from a trusted adult, like, Religious leaders, Mosque/Church, School Counselor, etc.- Rehabilitation- Mentorship- Reintegration.

B.   Become a Human Trafficking Fighter. Be a voice!!!

PART TWO

Influence Of Generational Gap

Chapter 8

Generational Gap: A Critical Factor in The Degeneration of Social Values in Christian Families And the Society.

I was interacting with a group of friends about some problems children feel they are facing in the family and how it could have been avoided if noticed earlier or certain measures taken. I began by telling them how I was having a strong conviction of late that families are not what they ought to be and that the society is suffering as a result of cutthroat competition, negative effects and acrimonious ways of living in most families today. It hurts a lot to see lives being destroyed and indeed it's sad to note that youths and teens are the most affected age group though the elderly also experience some level of pain. The rate of indiscipline has increased in our present day society and when an opportunity to interact with the parents on the subject arises, they always respond that it was not this way during their time, but all these changes occurred between the end of the 20th century and beginning of the 21st century. The major cause for concern is, if they are complaining about how things are now, then I wonder what their reaction will be some few decades down the line when things have grown worse. What values and morals will the next generation meet and how will they contend with the occurrences of their days? Then I ask myself, must we have to go back to the way of life of those years when things were commendable or simply adjust to the present century but using similar techniques used during those years? Something has to be done to help save this generation from further destruction or at least an effort should be made to

128

salvage it, resulting in a better and peaceful society. So I decided to consult as many people as I could to hear their different points of view on this issue and those contributions have formed a major part of this book.

"It is very common to hear elders complaining about the youth and the youths doing the same about the elders. No doubt there is tension between these two groups. Such divergence is capable of threatening the existence of the church and society at large." (Karimu Damap)

Generational gap is therefore the chasm that exists between the youths and the elders. The advanced learner's dictionary explains 'generation gap' as the "failure or inability of the younger and older generations to communicate and understand one another."

"Because of the intention of the elders to keep traditional norms intact and to maintain the status quo, new and helpful ideas brought by the youths are being shut out. There is little or no room for innovations and growth. Taking the spiritual sphere for example, the youths and children are regarded as fanatics when they want to express their spiritual gifts. This lack of free atmosphere to worship and to freely exhibit spiritual gifts is a major hindrance to full spiritual expression for the youths. As rightly stated by Karimu Damap, Church, societal and family growth is often hindered as a result of shutting out new ideas, this is both spiritual and numerical".

Ignorance on the causes and effects of behavioural changes in a child is one of the major key factors that affects our society. As a parent, have you ever asked yourself any of these questions? "Why is my child behaving this way lately? Why does my child love being indoors whenever others are in the living room? Why is my child not sharing issues when I can sense that he/she is depressed? Why is my child under-performing in school whereas he/she has had good grades in the past?" – What tends to be the problem?

Many parents in reality are too engaged with "other things" that some of these details don't seem important whereas the child tends to sense loneliness in their lives as a result of this neglect. This often leads to behaviours which are inappropriate, all in a way to substitute what they are missing in the family. Did you know that some children intentionally do some bad things just to gain attention which they have been deprived of for a long time? A close family relationship is one major area that cannot be negotiated. Its fruits do not just end at the family level, but even affect the peace and unity of a country; because whatever starts in the family becomes the expanse or replica the society faces.

Even though not all families are faced with these problems- relationships, negligence etc. Undoubtedly, most families are and perhaps many among them are already asking what they should do or what will be the way out. So, what I will be discussing in the next few sections are the common reasons why this happens and proffer some solutions on how this could be resolved. What does the word family mean? – Merriam Webster Dictionary defines family as the basic unit in society traditionally consisting of two parents rearing their children

Emphasis on the second definition here! It is a primary social group consisting of parents and children. But sadly, most families operate like a secondary social group where the deep relationship between parent and child is almost not there.

The problem with most parents is the wrong priority. A wise man once said, "Don't prepare the way for the child – Prepare the child for the road".

Most Parents, especially in Africa, and in Nigeria to be more precise, are so obsessed with preparing the road for their children. This includes, focusing on their education, buying them the best things available and saving up money for their future but they forget or neglect to groom the child. And usually the end result is the moral ills we are experiencing today. Moreover, that wealth hardly lives through to the third generation. Parents work so hard for the child but don't talk to the child. That in itself is a very dangerous way to live.

Having said all these, what then are some of the major causes of the ills experienced in the family?

Prayer and study of the Bible

Indeed, the family that prays together stays together. So the scripture rightly says in 2 Timothy 1:3 "pray without ceasing", meaning that no moment should pass a believer by without praying. It can be conscious or even unconscious but that must be the usual lifestyle for a believer and especially a parent. As parents today, I believe that you started learning how to pray from when you were toddlers, as this was a major practice in the preceding generation. You in turn now need to pass the same training to your children. Study of the Bible aids the child to meditate on God's promises so that when faced with difficult situations and challenges, the child can know through the help of the Holy Spirit how to respond by recalling some verses that he/she had been taught or studied. Unfortunately, most problems Christian homes face today are a result of negligence in the area of teaching their children how to independently study the Bible and pray and also, praying for their children. This not only grooms the child in facing life challenges but it also improves bonds that exist between the father, mother and children. A child should not be left to learn these basics on their own because the society around them is not modelling and upholding these values. Rather, they need guidance and this can't be done by anyone better than the parents who brought them into this world.

Communication

If in the organization we work and within the caucus of our contemporaries, communication is very important, then how much more in the family which is considered a primary social group where as a parent you have the obligation to bring them up in the right manner? There's a common cycle I see at play here in Nigeria and perhaps some other parts of the world; children enjoy closer relationship with their parents prior to and during the period when they are in primary school, but from the time they enrol in a secondary school, the parents begin to have limited time for their children and they spend more time trying to raise funds for the child's education. This is a critical stage in a child's development because it is when he/she begins to experience pre-adolescence, puberty, teenage and social changes etc. Hence, they need the appropriate platform or opportunity to discuss their experiences, feelings and challenges. It is also when children tend to begin rubbing off on one another and are forced into premature growth and maturity. Oftentimes, parents respond by getting furious that the child is stubborn and insubordinate. They expect the child to submit like a child but to behave like an adult emotionally and mentally. This often leaves the child confused, misunderstood and empty emotionally. As a result some of the children resort to smoking, drugs and alcohol and other ill-mannered behaviour of which the society prohibits the end result is much more devastating.

Before moving to the next point, I want to reemphasize that the greatest challenge and factor contributing to a broken parent-child relationship is lack of proper constructive communication. Communication is a wonderful bridge that cannot be done without. Parents need to remain emotionally connected to children to encourage good relationships.

Always remember that where prayer is valued there is unity, joy, peace, harmony, love will flow easily, comfort will not be lacking and with proper communication, understanding becomes easier. Family is not just about procreation but about living happily and fulfilling God's purposes. Love, attention and listening ears are vital things that most families lack today. All these three need to be administered effectively on the child considering his/her level of maturity. Hence taking one and giving in the other is risky for the development of a child's life in both the present and future aspects of their life.

When parents are not in good terms

Lack of unity among both parents when addressing certain behaviours among children is another factor that impacts their development. In the area of discipline for example, a parent may believe that the best way to correct a child is using the rod while the other parent may think it is inhuman to use a rod on a child. These conflicting ideas if not addressed can lead to serious problems. So I believe parents need to agree on what is morally correct and what is not, proper measures of discipline, responsibilities etc. which if not addressed has the capacity of creating tension in the home. Another extreme case is where both parents are not of the same faith or values and the children are forced into choosing between them. Believers are encouraged to guard against these kinds of unions, not only for their sake but for the children who will be born into these families.

If the other attitude either positive or negative - emotions, beliefs, and behaviours toward a particular object, person, thing, or event occurs in the family, then everyone knows that it could well be a result of poor relationship co-existing between the parents and it is most likely going to lead to divorce. All of these are in some way or the other a result of quarrelling, fighting and at times one parent tries to backslash on the favourite child of the other.

Nagging does more harm than good in the house. If a mother exhibits such character for example, the girl child sees that as a good thing and then practices it and in most cases, such children when married do the same and don't see giving appreciation to their spouse as a virtue.

In most cases children are left in a fix whenever there is a break in communication among their parents - at such times, whatever the outcome is, it bounces back on that child. That affects the spiritual life, growth and upbringing of children - children do as they please.

Words have a way of either playing the positive or negative roles in the life of a child. In terms of the negative, it makes children prone to negative thoughts which further deteriorates the child's morale and leads to low-self-esteem, because such a child thinks or perceives that even his/her parents don't have a positive thought towards him/her. This is dangerous because it always leads the child to depression. When parents are having personal issues, children are always at the receiving end. To parents, it leads to divorce or separation but mostly before that is done damage has already been done in the life and upbringing of their children.

'Marriage by correspondence'

It is defined as couples who are legally married but stay apart as a result of vocation, studies or other reasons. This results in only occasional visits by either husband or wife which are brief most times at weekends. The upbringing of children requires both parents to foster discipline in them. Mothers and fathers each have their definite roles in bringing up their children. Studies have shown that when children spend most of the time growing up with their mothers, they often have challenges in behaving in a respectful manner. This may not be true for all families but I believe it is for the great majority.

Lack of sufficient time

I often wonder, which of these is better? Should parents work and provide for the family or should parents stop working just to be with their family? Really it's not possible to substitute these two, because if parents don't work then the family will not have food, shelter, clothing, education etc. Most children whose parents are working, will prefer that they stop the work and take care of them

Work is important to both parents if needed, but it becomes bad when as a result, they don't have time for their families. Prior to this generation most parents only knew farming and so the father would leave their houses in the morning to their farms with the older male children while late in the afternoon the mother with the other older females would join them, bringing food, water, drinks etc. to help renew their strength. In this way, the family spent much time together and parents were the primary influences on their children. But things have changed today, there are many other areas for parents to work in. Let's suppose that you are a medical doctor as a father and your wife is also a medical doctor and both of you are working at different hospitals with similar work schedules. To cap it all, the children haven't grown up to understand what's happening. What do you think comes to their mind? That is if they are not bold enough to challenge you or discuss it outside with either their peers, teachers and surrounding neighbours whose children they mingle with? "See how you are always happy with your daddy or mummy, my mummy goes to work in the morning and returns in the evening"; or "sometimes, my father and mother fought yesterday, you need to see how my daddy beat my mum, she was bleeding badly and was rushed to the hospital this morning."

Let's now suppose that you came back home from work and still have more work to cover for the next day and your child comes with assignments so that you can help him/her out but you shout at the child because you have deadlines to meet, tell me how such a child would feel and think about you?Another scenario is when parents come in late, the mother goes in to cook dinner while the child is left in front of television programs & cartoons and the father goes out to hang out with friends and there are assignments from school undone for your child. I see this as a great opportunity for the father and mother to spend some time with the child, either in the kitchen or on their assignments or anything else that could be beneficial.

These are the kinds of situations which cause children to begin to meet new friends from different backgrounds to associate with and do the assignments with. And then all of a sudden, due to wrong associations, a child cannot be handled anymore and parents begin to move helter-skelter to proffer solutions in order to avoid being mocked by friends and colleagues. Though a child might not understand how busy your daily schedules are, he/she will surely benefit from that little time you give in the midst of your busy engagements as a father or mother. I always emphasize that a parent doesn't have to give a whole day each week to his children, but must learn to at least create a few days in the week to be around his/her family because this helps in building a healthy and loving home.

Being strict in the handling of children

Many times corrections are considered to be punishments or as an expression of hatred or dislike toward them. This is often so because children are not always told what they did wrong before being disciplined. On the other hand, some parents see leniency as being loose toward their children which results in disrespect. But discipline is correction and maintaining of standards and at the same time not compromising on certain rules and behaviour. To be strict on the other hand is to be firm. Parents ought to note that children obey their words and statements more than their expressions but the reverse is the case in many occasions as gestures, shouting, expressions of anger etc. dominate the act of correction. Age is an important factor which should be considered when discipline is administered. There are certain rules which parents really have to put into consideration for children of different age groups; not one single rule should apply to all. You must pray before eating and going to bed, always remember to kneel when greeting anyone who is older than you, always be a respectful child, keep companies or friends that will help you grow knowing who you are to those who will take you away from who you are meant to be and the likes of them. Talking about age, sometimes I feel that parents really don't know when their children have experienced a transition to pre-teen, teenager, youth or adult. So, they continue to treat their children the same way without realizing the changes that have taken place. This situation for the child is unacceptable because they now see themselves as grownups and demand respect. When this understanding is missing there is bound to be recurrence of disagreements on either side. On the other hand, when these changes are acknowledged, the frictions stated could be avoided.

Lack of Role Models

Embodying the character which you desire to instill in the life of your children is a very vital part of child training. These children need to see what you are saying, in your life and those who surround them in order for those words to register in their mind. So if there are compromises in the lives of the parents, the instructions given may not be so effective. Women are meant to be the bedrock of every house, and as it is rightly mentioned that "behind every successful house lies a woman", I will also add that "behind every successful home lies a mother", not just any mother but a woman who is ready to hold the family together at all cost and against her will if needed. If a mother is hardworking, she teaches not just the girls but even the boys to do likewise, if she is respectful then the children also imbibe the same character they have seen in their mum, if she is easily offended, she also passes on the same conduct to her children, if she is business oriented she tries to pass the same trait to her children at all cost. In fact, whatever she is and becomes, that's how her children and family become. A proud husband is always someone who looks back and has no other reason than to thank his wife for making him someone who is respected in the society (Proverbs 31:10-31). Though the teaching of moral conduct should not be on the shoulders of just one person, a mother has more roles to play in that aspect compared to the father. The moral behaviour a child gets in the family can determine how far he/she will go in life and so should not be taken for granted.

High rate of broken marriages

The unity of a family is vital to the upbringing and development of a child, and the moment it is tampered with, there is grave danger. Broken marriages play a fatal role in the disengagement of families which shouldn't be allowed to happen at any point in time because children always end up being victims.

As discussed above, when a child lacks parental care and advice, there is a higher tendency of living wayward and getting bad inputs from friends who wouldn't contribute positively into their lives. Some parents decide to stay together but really aren't living together and most of the time it's because of the children they have together.

Educationally, children from broken homes are robbed of the privilege to study well and sometimes they go to school very late and unkempt which leads to them being backward in their performances. They are also affected in their perception i.e. they begin to have the wrong mind-set that marriage is bad and full of trouble, void of love, full of violence and hatred.

Physically and emotionally, children are caught in the cross fires of parents who are not living in harmony. They suffer physical abuse, deprived of parental care and suffer some health issues both physically and emotionally. They often end up being aggressive as a system of defence against abuse and if left unchecked, it can affect them in their adulthood. Spiritually, there is no foundation to begin with for the pursuit of the knowledge of God while some resent spiritual things altogether.

Opposing children from using/actualising their dreams/talents/abilities

I really believe that parents need to be re-oriented on guiding and encouraging their children towards becoming who they want to be rather than causing them to neglect the area they love and can give their best into. Mostly the child obeys either out of fear or in order to please the parent.

When we look at the story of Jacob and Esau, they are two different personalities with different abilities. Isaac never discouraged Jacob from tending sheep nor did Rebecca discourage Esau from hunting. Both parents embraced the different abilities the two had and created an avenue for them to give their best. A child might not be good in the classroom but definitely, there is an area destined for this child to function appropriately. That doesn't mean education should not be given to a child, but there comes a time that it is secondary in the heart of the child compared to what he really intends to suit his/her destiny in life. The reason why most parents discourage their children from pursuing certain dreams/passion is either because they have not paid attention to what the child is best at or they weren't open to learning such. It is also possible that they have a mind-set issue regarding certain careers and don't want to shift from it.

Once children notice opposition, what comes next to their mind is fear. This ends in them forsaking their special abilities. Consequently, there will be a widening communication gap between children & the parents which is not desirable. Also, the child begins to avoid what could make them better and could be a blessing to others.

Once parents recognize special abilities, be it writing, business, entertainment, sports, athletics, whatever it might be, it is their duty to help the child develop in that area. Any parent who hasn't observed any special ability shouldn't frown at that child; rather, they should commit the child to

God in prayer for the discovery and full actualization of their gifts and destinies.

As a parent, you need to know that children are proud and respectful to those who encourage them during their life or stages of development. Sometimes it is so unfortunate to find out that those who champion the development of wonderful and great persons in society aren't immediate family members. Parents are mentors to their children in every field or area, character wise, attitude, spiritually, educationally, mentally and so on and by all means must stand by them in order to avoid emotional and psychological trauma that may threaten the child from fulfilling their assignment and purpose in life.

Children brought up by single mothers.

There is an increasing number of single mothers. Majority among them are teenage girls who had sexual relations that resulted in pregnancy and had to raise the child alone, being abandoned by the father of the child. This is commonly referred to as 'babies having babies' in some places. Similarly, there are matured women who do not want to get married but want to have children with whoever they choose and they are ready to take care of the children that they get as a result of such relationships. (As already discussed in previous sections, divorce or separation is a contributor to children raised by single mothers).

Apostle Johnson Suleiman once shared, *"I was a dignified cultist. I am from a home of separated parents. My parents had some issues. Any child from a home like that is bound to fall into the streets.*

"So, I got into school and I wanted acceptance somewhere. Someone told me that there is something called brotherhood and that I would be accepted as a family member and I liked it. I didn't know there was a beating part and being taken to the bush.

"I didn't like that. But you have to go into it. What I always avoided then was the assignments. I was just like a floor member.

I would go to meetings and when assigned to do something and I couldn't, I had to look for someone to do it and pay for it. I was not really happy but I was there." (www.naijanews.com)

Children raised by single mothers are more likely to fare worse on a number of dimensions, including their school achievement, their social and emotional development, their health and their success in the labour market. They are at greater risk of parental abuse and neglect, more likely to become teen parents and less likely to graduate from high school or college. Not all children raised in single parent families suffer these adverse outcomes; it is simply that the risks are greater for them.

One possibility is that children in two parent families do better because of the increased resources available to them. Single parents only have one income coming into the house. On top of that, single parents often have to spend a greater proportion of their income on child care because they do not have a co-parent to stay home with the child while they work. Even beyond having more income, two parents also have more time to spend with the child. A recent study by Richard Reeves and Kimberly Howard finds that parenting skills vary across demographic groups and that forty-four percent of single mothers fall into the weakest category and only 3 percent in the strongest category.

Differences of faith.

This is a scenario in which parents belong to different faiths or both may be Christians but attend different churches. This is often confusing to children because sometimes, the practices vary greatly and children find it difficult to know which one is which. In most cases, there are visible disagreements between parents that compound the problem. Such children may grow on a faulty spiritual foundation and some may resent spiritual things altogether

What Then Should Be The Way Forward?

The way a child is brought up

I always lay emphasis on this passage of the scripture that talks about training a child: Train a child in the way he should go, and when he is old he will not turn from it (Prov. 22:6 –NIV). Now this passage vividly talks about the age of learning/childhood to the age of maturity/adulthood. As a parent you will agree with me that the way a child talks when he/she is a toddler is not the same way he will talk at the age of 2 years and beyond. Everything is in stages and every stage must be valued as if it is the last in the development and upbringing of your child: Train a child in the way he should go, and when he is old he will not turn from it (Prov 22:6 -NIV). Apostle Paul further talked about this in 1 Cor 13:11, When I was a child, I talked like a child, I thought like a child, I reasoned like a child; now that I have become a man, I am done with childish ways and have put them aside. Quoting from the words of Pastor Chris Delvan, "At the stage of realization, the reverse is the case. It becomes 'now that I am a man, I reason like a man, think like a man, talk like a man and then behave like a man'. Now if parents realize that the major work in bringing up a child and transforming him into what they want him to be is from birth to the time he/she finishes university, then I believe that the family will have less problems with raising a child in the right manner.

Also, if the parents have issues to settle and the child notices it, chances are that either the child begins to practice what he sees at home with other children, or tries to deal with emotional trauma within him/herself. At times the child has the feelings of being unfortunate from the family he/she comes from, the moment they see other children spending time with their parents effectively.

The Family Altar

Indeed, the family that prays together stays together. As the scripture rightly says "pray without ceasing", meaning that no moment should pass a believer without him/her praying. It can be conscious or even unconscious but that must be the usual abode for a believer and most especially what a parent should be in. As a parent you may have started learning how to pray from when you were a toddler and then in turn, you now need to pass the same training to your children. Study of the Bible aids the child to meditate on God's promises so that in certain situations and challenges, the child can know how to overcome it through the help of the Holy Spirit.

Take them along

Most times, you see parents spiritually inclined towards God and perhaps even attaining great heights as a result of that, but their families are nowhere close to those achievements.

When David sensed that his successor was Solomon, He took his time to make Solomon understand leadership and how to achieve the heights he achieved as a father, but the opposite is the case in our days. Just as God has given you the grace to have certain spiritual understanding, He is also interested in your children benefiting from that grace. So parents, no matter your position in the society, you must learn how to put a balance to your growth and to that of your children.

Encourage them to live and achieve destiny

A common practice in African homes is a parent telling his/her child "don't do this" and stopping right there. To the child, most especially a teen who is approaching the age of puberty, that is not enough because at his/her age and level of development/understanding, the child needs explanation on the danger of choosing that career which to him/her counts and the importance of what he is being told to do should be clearly discussed. Summarily, what they need is guidance on why they should either go through that path or let it go so that when challenges arise along the chosen path, there won't be blame apportioned to parents. But when parents neglect this and stop at "don't do or go or live by it", children can be so determined to give it a try and find out why their parents are against that path. I am speaking from a personal experience, and at the end both parties suffer.

So if your child trusts you enough to discuss with you about a path he/she feels he wants to take to achieve destiny, all the child wants is your counsel and not judgment. It might interest you to know that if you give a good judgment, you will win the heart of the child on this particular subject and it will be difficult for someone else to convince him/her to back out of your counsel.

Creating time and space at all cost

Given the demands at the workplace in the present era, it becomes more difficult for parents to give adequate time and attention to the needs of their children and family. As I always say, it is not bad for a family to employ or have a help or maid which is a result of the tight schedule the parents find themselves in, but it becomes more dangerous when the help wins the heart of your ward, so that your ward no longer listens to you but can obey the instructions of your help or maid. The effect is often felt when the help is gone and you are left with your children and need to administer your former role and you find out that it is no longer possible. While some househelps assist your child to become good, many of them do more harm than good for you as the parent, to the child and to the entire family.

In other cases, instead of having the househelps, the children are left to cater for themselves. When they are back from school, they have the whole day to play with friends, watch television and any programme of their choice which is mostly cartoons while for those who are older, music of different kinds and movies become their hobbies. Since there is no proper supervision of the programmes, movies and the music they listen to, parents can at least spend the weekends with them, using such time to monitor what sort of entertainment the children have been indulging in during the week, because some of those programmes and music are evil and they go right into the spirit man of those children and begin to work negatively which later reflects in their behaviour later in life. Therefore, parents must learn and abide by this method if they really have the future of their child at heart. Times are proving impossible, but don't forget that they are your children and you asked for them. So, in the midst of the busy calls for duty and engagements you must create time also to attend to those needs that will help them in whatever way possible.

Children also learn by observing, and therefore parents must live exemplary lives for their children to emulate; otherwise they will master the wrong things and this will negatively affect them in future.

United in one faith

With the increasing number of worship centers/places all around, and parents holding on to different beliefs and teachings, children are really divided in their minds and choices, and that does much harm to their spirits, morality and even how they relate with people. I am not against parents attending different churches, but parents must be united in faith despite their different places of worship. Arguments, defenses and contradictions on doctrines should not be done by both parents in the midst of the children. It's harmful for the spiritual growth of that child and it also affects the manner in which they begin to see and think about those ministers/ministries being argued about. Just like the scriptures caution in 2 Timothy 2:23 "Don't have anything to do with foolish and stupid arguments, because you know they produce quarrels - NIV". At times I prefer the child choosing which side he/she wants to belong when he/she has come of age, but what about when they are still very young? The Apostle Paul said "there is one Spirit and one God", so I say there is no different way of prayer and reading of the word of God and worshiping God. Prayer is prayer everywhere, worship is worship everywhere, the Bible is the Bible everywhere and every minister can have his/her own interpretation but all should be to promote the spiritual growth of the believers. This also means you need to discern who you, as a parent, sit under for spiritual nourishment. A child should need to follow either of the parents for worship but as they grow up then they should be allowed to choose where they believe the Holy Spirit is guiding them to follow and with no obstruction; the fact that you were brought up in an Orthodox/Pentecostal/Evangelical setting does not mean that is the path for your child.

To conclude, I want to share the story of one of the greatest Kings of Judah, Hezekiah (2 Kings 20-21). He was one of the godly kings who ruled the people of God, at a point in time, he got sick and after receiving a word from God through the Prophet Isaiah, he prayed to God; and God added 15 more years to him after which he will join his ancestors. In the course of time, the scripture records that the King of Babylon sent representatives to come and greet him and to find out how he was faring and recovering.

Because he was happy with their visit, he decided to show the visitors all that was in his treasury, the gold, silver, diamonds, armory and the like; but God was not pleased and decided to call his attention to the mistake he made and because of which all that the Babylonians saw would be looted and his people made captives, even though not in his time as king. Amazingly, he was comfortable with that decision since it would not happen during his own time as king.

After his death, Manasseh his son succeeded him as King, but the fulfillment came during that time. He was the worst king that ever ruled Israel, to the extent of sacrificing his son; he became cruel and wicked, so that God had to vow not to wipe out his guilt due to those terrible and devastating things he did before the Lord.

This shows that no matter how good you are as a father, mother or a model, if you are not able to raise the next generation well, you might be termed as a failure, because the person coming after you will now undo all the good records and legacy you left behind.

King Hezekiah was focused on his own generation like most are now, without considering how to begin to work in helping the next generation get it better done. This calls for a need to be concerned about how the next generation success story will look like, no matter how good you are and how successful you have become, you will only be termed a success when you are able to model or raise someone to continue from where you stopped.

Chapter 9

Divorce: Its Impact On the Child

This chapter is written to help those who are going into marriage and those who are already married or are divorced or contemplating it, and highlights the dangers it portends to children under such circumstances. What comes to your mind as a believer when you hear of the word divorce? Should divorce be the last option when things go out of hand? What happened to the vows taken to stand by each other, to protect in sickness and health, life and death, riches or poverty, or was it that you later realized he/she was not the actual missing rib, that one woman you have prayed to spend the rest of your life with? In the whole scripture, God has always been against divorce, thereby making divorce to be an illegal practice, unless for extra-marital affairs stated in the scripture. Divorce has caused a lot of harm than good in the lives of the partners, children, immediate families and most especially the community, through the kind of habit children from these backgrounds turn out to become. Because, if parents are divorced, the child and his/her siblings are put in jeopardy.

What then is divorce?

Divorce is seen as the legal ending of marriage. While in my own opinion, what leads to divorce is when two people having different views out of God's initial plan for marriage and their lives, come together to try to make it work from their own human perspective. And when they realize it cannot work as they thought or planned or dreamed, they decide to give each other the chance to live happily once again. But in them living happily separately, they leave with

148

hurts and regrets on themselves as well hurt others in the process.

Marriage is an institution ordained by God and it has a special significance in our society. Obi (1990) defined marriage as a union between a man and a woman that lasts the duration of the man's life and the woman's life, as well as a social structure that promotes an association and agreement between two families. In other words, marriage is predicated on the mutual consent of a man and a woman to live together as husband and wife. Ordinarily, an ideal marriage will remain united, undivided, and unbroken. This was the plan written by the mind of the creator when He gave Eve to Adam as his permanent partner in the Garden of Eden.

Therefore, all efforts must be made to encourage couples to stay together or get back together, even when they have separated. It is therefore imperative that marriage be contracted for life or for an indefinite period. In spite of the significance of marriage, every society is faced with situations in which marriage fails and the couples cannot tolerate living together.

The aftermath of this is divorce. According to Grath (2001), divorce is a legal or customary decree that a marriage is dissolved, in other words, divorce is a permanent separation of married people as a result of an unexpected marriage outcome. Mbiti (2007.145) argues that Divorce is a delicate accident in marital relationships. What constitutes a divorce must be viewed against the fact that marriage is a process. In many societies that process is complete only when the first child is born, or when all the marriage presents have been paid or even when one's first children are married.

Once the full contract of marriage has been executed, it is extremely hard to dissolve it. In Nigeria as well as other parts of the globe, many divorced people remarry and about half of those who do are already parents. This results in the creation of "blended families" also called "stepfamilies".

Before we go forward on this matter of divorce, but with focus on its effect on the child, let's hear the stories also of victims who were unlucky to have such an encounter and what really happened.

"I've been in that shoe of a divorced person or parent for almost 14 years now, that was around 2006," she said. And the cause behind the separation was because I bore female children, 4 in all. The separation was supposed to be in the mid-eighties, after I gave birth to my second daughter; my father-in-law came and asked, you gave birth to another female child again? Better let her go, he informed my husband. But my ex-husband could not, because he was still studying, was doing his Diploma Programme at the Kaduna State Polytechnic, of which I was the sponsor.

His father kept mounting pressure on him to divorce me, he refused to oblige to those demands at first, considering the study he is currently enrolled in coming to an end, because all he ever needed, I stood by him through that time. After completing the Diploma Programme, he enrolled for his H.N.D (Higher National Diploma) programme again and then proceeded for his Post Graduate Studies; then around 2005/2006 he asked me to leave. But in 2006, he officially served me a letter of divorce; on that fateful morning, he led the family devotion and then called me with my name, I responded, and he summoned me to the sitting room and brought out a white envelope, addressed with my name and father's name, after collecting it, I opened it and read the content inside; then I knelt down before him and thanked God, I also thanked him, telling him, today you finally fulfilled what has been in your heart all these years, and I have received the letter in good fate.

After giving me the letter, he said three things that made him give me the divorce letter – 1. He has been enslaved so much. 2. He needed progress and 3. He needs freedom. Within me, I began to think that I have enslaved him and have denied him the chance and opportunity to progress and maybe have restricted him from certain things where he never had freedom. But earnestly speaking, if anyone ever cared to ask why he took the decision he did, it would be because I gave birth to female children. People begged him, asking him to withdraw, even the children who were crying and asking him to reconsider the decision, but it all proved abortive with him telling them he cannot keep two wives. Saying I have to go so that he can bring in someone who can give him male children. At the moment, with the second wife also, God blessed them with two female children too.

There are so many causes of divorce, but mine was because I had female children. With his father in support of that, he never had regard for them as his children, calling them useless children/gifts cannot amount to anything. But reverse is the case now, they have become the bread winners of the family; so that when the same grandfather who never liked them passed away on the 29th of April, they took responsibility of all the burial arrangements, with their father only sourcing for ambulance and fuelling his car and settling the mortuary bill.

So, as a single or divorced mother, if you are not close to God, it leads to more chaos in the family, which ends up affecting the children; because separation came. I really appreciate my spiritual father who stood by me with words of encouragement after I took the letter to him. With an assurance from him that I will own my house before he will be transferred, but I was thinking of where to get finance to build the house. God in his greatness made that come to pass in 2008. He advised me to look for a room and start with, but ensure that I am close to my children, always visiting them, and them visiting me as well. By that, I will be able to know if he can take care of the children I left behind or not, and I did that. Squatted with a church member for one and half years and then the fulfilment of the house came. Surprisingly, even after the whole experience, I still cook food from my house and still take to the children; when they cook with his new wife, they will not give some to the children, if they will give them any food, it's always a stale one, no school fees or pocket money to help them educationally. My first daughter was in NCE 2 at that time, the second just got admission in a College of health. He denied them of many things a father should have provided to his children.

Just to mention some few causes of divorce: Marital Unfaithfulness, barrenness, pressure from in-laws due to the inability of the woman giving birth, parents encouraging their daughters to go for divorce because of the husband's status and giving birth to female children instead of male.

After the whole thing, I thought of withdrawing myself from people due to the negative information reaching me which was not true, and some husbands were scared of permitting their wives associate with me thinking I will influence them negatively, I also had issues with finance. Some went to rent a house and were denied because they were divorced, life is actually a difficult one to divorce parents and most especially women. Feelings of being lonely and rejection were some challenges, it was difficult for people to now trust me, thinking it was my character/behaviour that led to the divorce, but I was the only one who knew exactly what had happened. At times wrong judgement from people also acts as a bad omen on those who face divorce.

My kids suffered a lot; people were pointing fingers at them, calling them names and not regarding them as part of their immediate community, they lacked the trust of people around, and they almost constantly lived in fear of what people would say or do to them as a result of what happened. In some cases, when a daughter was betrothed to get married, upon hearing what happened, some of them always withdraw and call the marriage plans off, believing the fate of their mother can also happen to them.

To the children; just like the mother, the children equally have to be strong and have to put their faith in God, believing him to either work through reconciling their parents or accepting their fate and trusting him to guide them on what to do and how to live different and better lives from their parents.

Though it was difficult, I had to put my trust in God to help me not to encounter harassment from men who will want to take advantage of my situation, and indeed he has equally been faithful there as well.

My advice to intending parents/couples, those newly married and those who are currently facing a case like mine is to be faithful because it is very important. Lean unto God and be prayerful, that's the only thing that will help you. Going to seek for other means out of God will further make matters worse, and always ensure to study your bible, and in most cases share it with your spiritual head; and as a woman obey your husband as the scripture rightly states. That's my general advice to them.

Like I earlier mentioned, unless in the case of unfaithfulness, a man or woman are not permitted to think towards divorce. The Bible states this clearly in the Book of Matthew 19:7-9 **"they said to him, why then did Moses command to give a certificate of DIVORCE and thus to dismiss and repudiate a wife? He said to them, because of the hardness of your hearts, Moses permitted you to dismiss and repudiate and divorce your wives; but from the beginning it has not been so. I say to you: who ever dismisses his wife, except for unchastity, and marries another commits adultery, and he who marries a divorced woman commits adultery"** (Amplified Version). Also, another place in the scripture has stated clearly, **"therefore a man shall leave his father and his mother and shall BECOME UNITED and CLEAVE to his wife, and they shall become ONE FLESH"** – Genesis 2:24; the Message Translation **stressed "and because of this, a man leave father and mother and is firmly bonded to his wife, becoming one flesh – no longer two bodies but one" Matthew** 19:5. All these scriptures have one thing in common, BECOMING ONE FLESH, which shows that once the two have agreed to stay together, professing the marital vows there is no separation of any kind, unless for marital unfaithfulness.

People always wonder what leads to most divorce. Oftentimes, people look at the physical features of either the man or woman without considering what the ultimate plan of God is in Marriage. Because there is no way you can think of God's ultimate plan for you and your partner and settle for divorce; remember God is a giver of good gifts, which tells us that "all good gifts" comes from God, and they add no sorrow to it. Parents, the moment you think of divorce, have you ever asked yourselves what God's ultimate plan actually was?

Even though divorce has existed from the beginning of times, but looking at the patriarchs in the Bible, you will know that God has been an amazing companion even in marriage; because the marriage between a man and a woman is a replica between our marriage with him, here on earth before the completion of it in heaven. So when divorce becomes the last resort, you are not just separating yourself from your physical companion ordained by God, but equally from your maker.

Our concentration in this subject is not on parents and why they did what they did, but on the innocent child/children who are now left broken with parents living separately.

It raises unanswered questions in the hearts and minds of these children with a world torn apart, and the confusion of what to do and where to start from; all of these clouds their minds, and mostly at a young age.

The pride of a child is seeing his/her parents living happily; and his greatest woe is realizing or knowing that the once happy home he knew will no longer be, this has nothing to do with the years of marriage. So, I dare to say, Divorce is a mind-set also.

For instance, in 1992, over 11% of all American children were living with one biological parent and one step parent. Estimates are that a fourth of American children will live with a step parent before reaching the age of sixteen (Cherlin and Furistanbery, 2000). In the same vein, Nigeria in recent years has witnessed a high rate of divorce as a result of urbanization and industrialization (Adegoke, 2010). The periods triggered monetary industrial economy. Thus, the extended family that used to resolve conflicts or misunderstanding between couples no longer function effectively like in the past. The extended family structure eventually broke-up in the process; and there was a shift towards the nuclear family system characterized by less involvement of members in the resolution of marital conflicts.

It can be argued that perhaps the most important factor in the increase in divorce throughout the twentieth century has been the greater social acceptance of divorce. In particular, this increased tolerance has resulted from relaxation of negative attitudes toward divorce among various religious denominations. Although, divorce is still seen as unfortunate, it is no longer treated as sin by most religious leaders (Gertel, 1997). Many states including Nigeria have adopted more liberal divorce laws in the last two decades.

Divorce has become a more practical option in newly formed families, since they now tend to have fewer children than in the past. Adegoke (2010) observed that the search for employment by family members in the labour market or their inability to find work can be considered as a disruptive force in maintaining marital stability. More so, a general increase in family income coupled with the availability of free legal aid for some poor people, has meant that more couples can afford the traditionally high legal costs of divorce proceedings.

It is also believed that, as society provides greater opportunities for women, more and more wives are becoming less dependent on husbands economically and emotionally. They feel more able to leave on their own if the marriage seems hopeless. Divorce will continue to be on the increase in Nigeria if its causes and effects are not properly identified and controlled.

In the past decades, the rate of divorce in Nigeria was very minimal. Husbands andwives knew that marriage was contracted to keep the family genealogy going. Moreover, both husband and wife knew their roles in the family. More importantly, in Nigeria, marriage was never regarded as an individual affair. The family members had much influence on what went on in the family.

However, these trends changed overtime when people became increasingly individualistic and took the laws into their own hands. This was the time that family values started eroding, which eventually resulted in an increase of divorce in contemporary society.

"My family was very religious growing up and when the divorce happened, I lost that religious framework in my life. I saw my family as a sacred entity and then it was shattered."

"I felt the vows that they made before their families and God were violated and they now meant nothing."

"I am Catholic and I believe in God. I went through my parents' divorce when I was 5 years old and now I am going through another with my mom and step father at age 20. I believe God has a plan but it is hard to convince yourself when such tragedy occurs."

(Warner, 2007).

As these quotes from college students vividly illustrate, parental divorce can shatter a child's beliefs in the sanctity of his or her family, and faith can become an added source of suffering at a time when solace is needed. National surveys also highlight that parental divorce can drive wedge between youth and organized religion. For example, youth whose parents' divorce less often attend religious services and participate in religious classes, bible study groups, or church activities compared to youth from intact families (<u>Milevsky & Leh, 2008</u>; <u>Zhai, Ellison, Glenn, & Marquardt, 2007</u>). Likewise, youth from divorced families often switch to a different religious denomination or describe themselves as not belonging to any religious denomination compared to youth whose parents remain married (<u>Lawton & Bures, 2001</u>).

Further, most youth live through parental divorce without depending on their religious community. For example, according to the National Survey on the Moral and Spiritual Lives of Children of Divorce (NSMSL), about 75% adolescents of divorced parents recalled that no one from their church, neither clergy nor laypeople, had reached out to them when - the divorce occurred (<u>Marquardt, 2005</u>). Many adolescents may also distance themselves from their religious community to avoid feared or actual criticism on religious grounds about their parents' divorce (<u>Zhai et al.,2007</u>).

These processes may contribute to the fact adolescents' self-image often shifts from being "religious and spiritual" to "spiritual but not religious" after parental divorce (<u>Zhai, Ellison, Stokes & Glenn, 2008</u>). Thus, parental divorce can precipitate a second silent, yet quite painful, dissolution - namely a schism between the child and his or her religious community of origin.

What causes divorce then?

Childlessness: this goes back to the definition of divorce I gave. As much as having children in marriage is key, it is always difficult for couples or married people to live without hearing the cries and noise of children in the house called their own. African culture has prioritized children as an achievement, to the extent that when you are not blessed with them, it causes a lot of trouble between the woman and her husband, and the immediate in-laws. In all, when the couple are able to know the ultimate goal of God in their marriage, it will not be a problem for them to stay without children and still live happily; and in some cases go for the option of adoption which can equally be of help.

In addition to this, some causes of this childlessness, might not be from the woman as presupposed, it might be that the man is suffering from a sickness making it difficult for him to perform as a man, but the culture will not look at the man as the one with the fault, but the innocent woman. While in other cases, the woman might actually be the cause; have undertaken abortion which has caused the damage of her womb amongst other causes of childlessness.

Quarrelling: one thing about quarrelling and fighting between married people is the fact that it mostly occurs in the presence of the children, which further passes a negative thought to the children about the beauty that lies in marriage, leading to a lot of negative behaviours practiced by the children later on in life. As another cause, either of them can end up with scars that are very visible to everyone. In such cases, it becomes difficult to keep the marriage moving. So divorce can also become the last option.

Alcoholism/Drug Abuse: Alcoholism and related substances and quarrelling have the same impact on the family most times. Once a father prefers drinking to his family, it becomes difficult for him to prioritize the need of his family over alcohol. This makes the family always in need, but with less to cater for the family and the mother always tries hard to cater for the family, and such fathers always end up beating the mother and at times the children. Such fathers make demands that they have not really put in place; in such cases, it takes a mother who thinks of her children and the bigger plans to still remain in that marriage; most times, the mother leaves the house broken and the children broken as well.

Alcoholism in marriage is not a practice by fathers alone but also some mothers, but mostly practiced by fathers. Most of those men don't keep one wife, and can never be a good example to their children. If things must actually change in our present day society, a lot has to be done in the restoration process; in as much as it is possible, it needs every parent to first work on him/herself then it will be possible for the family to be restored and then the larger society too.

Socialization and Technological Advancement

Modern society is dynamic. Most

families in Africa are highly influenced by social activities, mass communication techniques, and community friends (Obi, 1990). These factors could pose dangers in some homes.

The home should protect its members against undue influence of friends and neighbours. Couples should not allow anyone who does not belong to the family circle to exert excessive influence on the family, or feel the right to influence family affairs, or be too familiar with the family. Some friends may be wolves in sheep's clothing; they may be pretending to be friends but in actual fact, they may have some ulterior motives— at times, familiarity breeds contempt. When there is too much familiarity between a spouse and a friend, the friend may become a threat to family solidarity. The female children may be a temptation to a male family friend.

Further, prolonged contact in an atmosphere that stimulates the senses may become dangerous for the husband or the wife. In most cases, before married couples realize what is going on, it has become too late. Couples are advised to avoid any rift that may bring disunity and quarrel in their relationship. This will help to reduce the rate of divorce, which is increasing at an incredible rate in Africa.

Financial Difficulties: Being married to a man/woman who comes from a poor family makes the partner who comes from the wealthy family want to take control of what happens in the house; who says what and how things must be done. So if the wealthy one is talking, the other partner must keep quiet and listen. Overtime, it creates crack, pride steps in, nagging, claiming of right and who is in charge of the house, no agreement when it comes to sex life, and many other negative things follow. Marriage is a union which has no thought about your family background, all it thinks about is how the two of the opposite sex must grow as one. Unless that is done, it always leads to breakup.

In some other cases, parents are equally another cause of divorce. They ask their children; what does he have that he can feed you with? What did you see in this poor boy/man, when the children of other wealthy people approached you, you said no to them only to agree to this poor boy just to suffer? Leave him alone and come back home, we have enough to feed you with, after all you have never lacked while at home. See how you have become slim and tattered. They give negative information or advice that the girl gets fed with overtime and equally deny her from seeing the bigger picture, but considering the current state decides to work with it, and in no time divorce takes place.

Immaturity: Age at marriage is one of the leading factors in divorce. It seems that it is best not marry too young or wait too long before marrying. Women who marry while still in their teens are twice as likely to divorce as women in their thirties. But those who marry in their thirties are half again as likely to divorce as those who marry in their twenties (Komblum 2001).

It has been observed that higher ages at marriage are typically thought of as an indicator of female autonomy. Age at marriage is often found to have a considerable positive effect on marriage stability, both in a western context and African population (Martin and Burm pass 1989; and Reiners 2003). But Isiugo-Abanihe (1998) did not find a significant effect of age at marriage on marriage stability decreasing with an increasing age at marriage. The age at which many modern couples marry has seriously been questioned.

In the lgbo traditional society, couples get married at a matured age. Age greater than eighteen is considered to be a mature age for women. However, this trend has changed dramatically in modern Nigerian society. Many broken families have been associated with the immaturity and youthfulness of the married couple who get married in their teens (13-17). Marrying too young is destructive and has a tremendous impact in a relationship. Some youths are not experienced enough to face the realities of life. As a result, it is no wonder that the rate of divorce linked to youthful marriage is high. Rhyme (2010) argued that the biggest factor in marital disharmony is immaturity. In Nigeria for example, going by the generally expressed rarity of divorce in traditional Yoruba setting, the present tendencies in marital dissolution among women in metropolitan Lagos is considered sociologically significant.

For instance, divorce and separation have been shown to be on the increase as a result of education and urbanization (Adedokun 1998), the incidence of remarriage is relatively high among the women of reproductive age. Thus, she stressed the point that all first marriages and most second marriages took place before the women were 40 years old and obviously still within their reproductive years.

Effect Of Divorce On The Child

In the midst of all of these crises that is rocking the family apart, there sits an innocent soul whose mind, if already developed or still developing, is left to begin to think of what is happening and try to come to a logical conclusion to why this should happen? In most cases, some decide to accept fate as it has come, while others it is now a scar that sticks with them and most end up transferring the aggression to innocent partners who might want to help rebuild the broken/cracked walls. Let us now consider some of the effects on a child:

Spiritual effect: When you come across these kinds of children, they always have one question when you try telling them about the existence of God. Where was God when my mum and dad were separating? If he really exists, why will he allow them to separate and put me in this condition? Many of them find it very difficult to put their trust in God, they leave with a broken spirit which equally takes the intervention of God to get a suitable partner who will help mend those broken walls caused over time.

They equally go through life with a clouded judgement and an unforgiving spirit; because as they grow, each side will want to explain what led to the separation and the parent who is at fault is now seen as the bad person with children never having regard for him/her, leading to a life of unforgiveness. Spiritually they have been destabilized, and then it manifests in the physical with very negative results.

Behavioural effect: A child who lives with his/her parents always believes that he will be protected whenever anything or issue arises; but the reverse is the case with a child from a divorced home. These children tend to be violent; all in a way to protect themselves from all sorts of harassment, they just believe life cannot and should not be handled the easy way, if not they will have a lot of troubles, so in order to have a hedge they prefer to be that way. Most of them also yield to negative pressure as another way to protect themselves from their peers.

Educational effect: It is almost difficult to ascertain the future of such a child educationally. If the parent values education, then it becomes helpful, however, if the unlucky child is either sent to hawk, become househelp, or any sort of menial jobs, it becomes disastrous. So the child learns hardship and responsibility at a very young age, with such a child's future on the line, his peers now have better opportunities above him or her in almost every aspect.

Sexual harassment: This is mostly faced by the girls, if the girl now stays with the father, the father might want to take advantage of her and begin to engage in sexual intercourse with the daughter. Of late, the rate of child molestation and harassment between fathers and their children has been on the increase, and the reason is mostly because of these broken homes. Most mothers, after leaving the house, do not return to check how the children are faring, thereby, exposing them to any form of attack. So it's either the father taking advantage, or a close relative, and when she refuses she becomes a victim of rape, and now lives with more pains and hurts with no one to open up to. But when a mother always keeps close touch, the daughter can open up to find help.

Societal effect: The children are now exposed and vulnerable to all sorts of abuses and negative words thrown at them, leading them to a life of obscurity most times. Some of them find it difficult to now associate with their peers, except the one they are welcome to; as parents are facing the hurt and societal rejection due to the action, the children are having more of it. Adults might have a strong heart to manage the pressure thrown at them as a result of divorce, but for that child, he/she has it very difficult. It takes real time for them to now adapt to the new world they have, and they need to comprehend and fit into it as well.

What's the way out?

God's intention for man has always been to love and be loved. And the moment that circle is broken, it leads to a lot of disaster and pain. In as much as divorce is not a welcomed idea and should never be, it is gradually becoming an acceptable law practiced most especially in the western countries, with Africa gradually picking up. Thereby sending the wrong message that in a couple of years to come, we will have more divorced homes to godly homes.

How can we cope with divorce then?

1. Prayer: It has been an established fact in marriage, that whenever a family prays together, they grow together spiritually and physically, and they learn to wave aside the faults of one another. Prayer is key, not just in marriage, but this has to start from the relationship days moving into the marriage. Prayer conquers all things, that seems to be impossible.

2. Love: Love equally conquers all things. Love keeps wrongs aside and consider the good of the other; with love, mountains that seem too difficult to climb become easier. With love comes happiness, peace, joy and fulfilment, and once a family is devoid of that, divorce will always be an option. Love also has a way of respecting one another irrespective of the background, all that matters is what will make you both live happily.

3. Faithfulness: If a man/woman actually loves his/her husband/wife, irrespective of the beauty or pressure from other ladies or external force due to an argument that ensued between them, both he/she cannot take advantage of that to hurt the feelings of the other. That becomes another reason why prayer should never depart from a family, especially newly married couples who are trusting God for better days together.

4. Friends and Influence: This is usually common with women. Your friend, be it married or still single, should not determine how to make your marriage work, because problems in marriage differ. What will work for one will not work for another; you must learn to shut your ears to all sorts of influence, except if you have a friend who is willing to stand with you on her knees to pray along with you, strengthening you all through the way. As much as women are key, men are not left behind; friends will equally want to use you as bait to destroy your marriage. When you took the oath it was for you two to enjoy your marriage and not someone telling you how to, so the moment other people begin to tell you or decide for you how to make your marriage work, especially when this influence is negative, flee away from such people. Instead of you being happy, you will be hurt and end up regretting your action towards your partner.

5. Guidance and counselling: When things go sore, sometimes it is advised that you not share with family or friends, but with the person who serves as your spiritual head. He who is filled with the spirit of God and wisdom can either call you both and speak to you, or you alone; telling you what he/she believes can restore your home and marriage from collapsing. Most partners bridge this step and decide to take laws into their own hands, and that's why it is sometimes possible for spiritual people to really be of help when the matter has gone out of hands.

6. Think of the big picture: Big picture regarding your child. Whatever decision you take at such a key moment really determines the future of the child. Even though some parents strategize ways and means on how to help the child, it is not the best. He needs you all, the love, care, protection, attention and the likes. It is almost always difficult for a child raised by a single parent to make it through the journey, except he/she has a strong spiritual parent to put him through, guiding him/her towards what to do.

7. Campaign and enlightenment: The government and other religious related organizations should think of seminars, workshop that will involve both married, newly married couples and intended married couples. Each couple should sit under the guidance of those who have stayed long and happily married for years with godly experience and examples to hold their hands and teach them from life experiences and scripture on what it actually means to have a happy home. By doing that, it will greatly reduce the rate of divorce. This should equally be applied in Muslim settings, because they equally experience a high rate of divorce compared to the Christian setting.

Divorce is not just faced by one particular setting, it is a global issue/problem that has caused a lot of havoc and pain in the lives of so many, leaving the victim with hurts and regrets at most times. This is a problem that everyone must put their hands on deck to fight parents, pastors and imams, the couples, the government, and organizations. I really do not believe that there is no problem without a solution, but one must be willing to accept the solutions and give it a try. Most marriages fail majorly because of lack of understanding; it all looks rosy in the beginning, but just after encountering one problem, none of the partner recalls the vows taken, everyone begins to apportion blame on the other, no one is willing to reconcile, forgetting the good glorious moments encountered during friendship and relationship days. One other solution is to stop considering the present state of your partner, there is always a little beginning, but the end is what counts. I have seen and heard many stories of couples who started with almost nothing, but the love that had sustained them to where they are today.

Considering the current state and seeing that nothing good will come out of this is a wrong perspective, at times God actually wants you to work as a team to grow to the position he wants you to reach. In God it is always teamwork while with the enemy it is always self. So, whenever severe issues arise, instead of thinking of divorce as the last resort, can you think of these two factors and consider? 1. What God's ultimate plan is in the midst of the trouble surrounding you and why did he permit it to come your way? 2. If divorce becomes the last option, what is the fate of the innocent child you gave birth to, will he/she be strong enough to withstand all the darts that come his way like you will? Will he/she be able to cope after the separation?

PART THREE

Handling The Challenges Of Adolescence

Chapter 10

Handling Teenage Pregnancy and Abortion

What comes to your mind when you realize your child, girlfriend or the doctor tells you- you or your partner or your child is pregnant? What's your first reaction as a parent, boyfriend and the girl?

Teenage pregnancy is a rampant phenomenon or occurrence in society, and mostly as a result of peer pressure. More than anything in the world, choices of friends determine the quality and direction of your life.

What is teenage Pregnancy?

Teenage pregnancy or adolescent pregnancy is when a girl under the age of 20 or in her teens gets pregnant and gives birth or aborts. Teenage/adolescent pregnancy is a global problem which has its consequences on health, social and the economy.

As a teen, the body is still in the process of maturity biologically, and so it's not fit for a change such as pregnancy. So if a girl gets pregnant at that age, it places her and the baby at high risk of ill-health conditions such as eclampsia, puerperal endometritis and systemic infections compared to a woman who is above the age of 20.

Every year, an estimated 21 million girls aged 15–19 years in developing regions become pregnant and approximately 12 million of them give birth. At least 777,000 births occur to adolescent girls younger than 15 years in developing countries.

The estimated global adolescent-specific fertility rate has declined by 11.6% over the past 20 years. There are, however, big differences in rates across the regions. The adolescent fertility rate in East Asia, for example, is 7.1 whereas the corresponding rate in Central Africa is 129.5. There are also enormous variations within regions. In 2018, the overall adolescent fertility rate in South-East Asia was 33. Rates, however, ranged from 0.3 in Democratic People's Republic of Korea to 83 in Bangladesh.

And even within countries there are enormous variations. In Ethiopia, for example, the total fertility rate ranges from 1.8 in Addis Ababa to 7.2 in the Somali region, with the percentage of women aged 15-19 who have begun childbearing ranging from 3% in Addis Ababa to 23% in the Affar region.

While the estimated global adolescent fertility rate has declined, the actual number of child births to adolescents has not, due to the large – and in some parts of the world, growing – population of young women in the 15–19 age group. The largest number of births occur in Eastern Asia (95,153) and Western Africa (70,423), and in Nigeria.

Adolescent pregnancies are a global problem occurring in high, middle, and low-income countries. Around the world, however, adolescent pregnancies are more likely to occur in marginalized communities, commonly driven by poverty and lack of education and employment opportunities.

Several factors contribute to adolescent pregnancies and births. In many societies, girls are under pressure to marry and bear children early. In least developed countries, at least 39% of girls marry before they are 18 years of age and 12% before the age of 15. In many places, girls choose to become pregnant because they have limited educational and employment prospects. Often, in such societies, motherhood is valued and marriage or union and childbearing may be the best of the limited options available.

Before we go any further, let's read the stories or experiences of some people who were bold enough to share, keeping the pregnancy until they gave birth; and later hear that of others who equally had difficulty keeping the pregnancy and why, and their regrets as well.

Teenage Pregnancy

> The story of a young girl who became a mum when she was still a teenager

Pregnant at the age of 15 and ready to share - this is the story of a young girl who became a mother when she was still just a teenager herself.

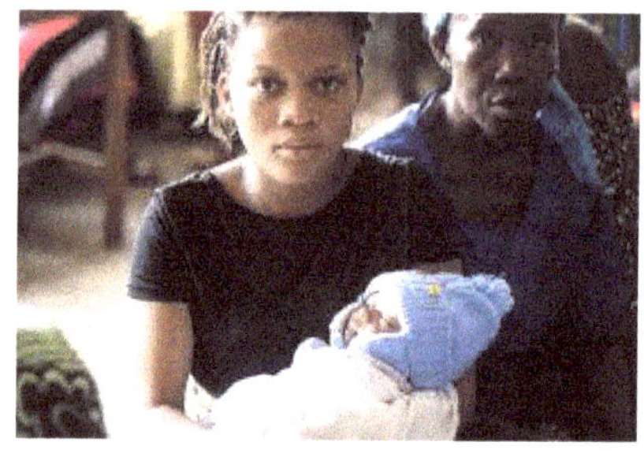

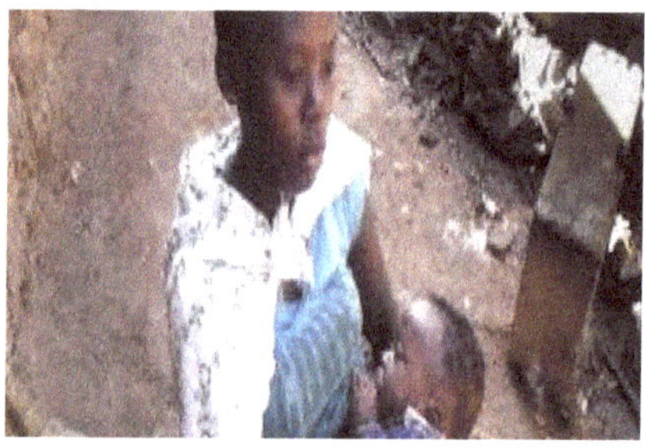

Two years ago I was a normal, fun-loving, school-hating teenager. I wasn't the most well behaved student. I answered back. I hated authority. I drank a fair bit but I was friendly. I loved my family, my friends and my boyfriend.

On the 8th of August 2008, I was in Queensland with my family and boyfriend celebrating our one-year anniversary. Two months later my entire life fell apart.

I had a massive fight with my best friend, Annie. This fight divided our group of friends who, to me, were more like family than just friends. My boyfriend sided with me and his best mate, Warren, sided with Annie and the rest just fell away.

➢ I was pregnant and didn't know what to do

I was also trying to deal with the fact I was <u>pregnant</u> and didn't know what to do. When I told my boyfriend he looked at me and asked, "What are we going to do?"

His response meant the world to me. Most boys our age in the same situation would ask, "What are you going to do?"

My boyfriend and I kept my pregnancy a secret between ourselves. We looked up <u>abortion clinics</u> because at the time I knew I didn't want a baby. I had a good life. I drank, laughed, I was a <u>teenager having a lot of fun</u>.

Eventually I found a clinic in the city, only to discover that because sex isn't legal until 16, neither is abortion. In order to go through with the abortion, I had to convince a counsellor I was mature enough to know what I was doing, which I did.

We made an appointment for five days before Christmas. I anxiously waited for a referral to arrive in the mail from the hospital.

Unfortunately, it arrived on a day that I wasn't watching over the letterbox. My mum saw the letter, opened it and started to sob. She called my dad, then my boyfriend's mother, and then the rest of his family knew. His sister wasn't impressed and name-calling occurred. A whole family drama erupted - it's still not quite repaired, and may never be.

I missed my appointment at the abortion clinic. I don't know how or why. Maybe I was scared, or maybe I just knew deep in my heart that I didn't want to go through with it. I never talked about it. I just continued on with my pregnancy knowing that I would either keep the baby, or give it up for adoption.

Two days after my 16th birthday, I went to have an ultrasound and was told it was a boy. My heart broke. I was sure I was having a girl. I cried for weeks. Eventually, I adjusted to expecting a boy. It took a while to get used to.

I enrolled in school from home and completed whilst pregnant.

During a routine appointment in June, I was admitted to hospital for pre-rupture of membranes. The next morning, I was induced and by that afternoon my baby boy, Oliver, was born.

I felt uncomfortable in the hospital. I didn't like being left alone with Oliver, not knowing what to do. He also had <u>club foot</u> so that meant more doctors coming in and out, asking me questions.

The first two months were really difficult. I felt like I didn't like my baby at all, and then without realizing it was happening I fell in love. I loved him so much, I would do anything for him. He was a little bundle of smiles who loved me unconditionally.

Whilst he was still a newborn, I continued to complete my school. At the start of the year he went into care four days a week so I could continue schooling. My friendships changed a lot. I still miss Annie sometimes. My friends still expected me to be the same person I was before I had Oliver. I still am that same person, but I'm different at the same time. I'm a mother. I feel I was born to be a mother.

My partner is such a loving father. He finds it difficult at times, but I think it's because I live with Oliver and my partner doesn't.

In public I get odd looks from people - often people will call me names, but I know the truth. I've slept with just one person, and he's the father of my child. Most people are surprised that I'm still at school and doing so well.

Motherhood is not easy for anyone, but I enjoy it now. I love when he hugs me and gives me huge smiles and giggles, and his chattering. I don't think I'm your average teen mum. I pride myself on being responsible, and being polite.

I wouldn't suggest that anyone get pregnant as a teen, but it is actually not the end of the world. It's the start of a life. I love my son; I do what is best for him. He is a beautiful boy who is loving, caring and I hope he'll stay that way.

People who judge me aren't very understanding. There are good and bad mothers of all ages. I'm a good mother, and I'm young. My son is happy, and has the smiles to prove it.

> It started during my final year at secondary school, before my JAMB I found out I was pregnant; I was sad and broken I cried a lot because I was scared of facing society and my family.

A lot of people said awful things about me, I lost a lot of friends, rumours were spread about me, negative talks, things I didn't even do were believed that I did. I had to fight myself not to give listening ears to what they said so I'd not get hurt more, even though it was hard, it was a decision I chose to make so no one could question my actions.

I met this pastor at school, I told him I was pregnant and he encouraged and advised me that he'd help me with the help of God. So that was how I was convinced to keep the baby. I feel really happy, motherhood is a thing of joy and I am glad I am experiencing mine now, even though it wasn't planned but still, I don't regret my actions.

I'd encourage youths to abstain from sexual immorality, in as much as the body craves for the opposite sex, we need to discipline ourselves and adhere to the doctrine or teachings we've been taught both at home, school and church. It's not for anybody's safety, but for ours.

> ➢ Back then at home, I was always locked down after my graduation; so I had no freedom of getting to know how the outside world actually looked like. So when I got admission, I thought this was my opportunity to be free and explore the world. So I got a boyfriend, and one thing led to another I got pregnant.

I was pregnant for over 6 months, but I didn't even know about it, you might want to ask how? I was not seeing my menstrual period/cycle, so I complained to my mum, and she said maybe it's an infection; we went to the hospital and when a test was carried out, it was confirmed that it was an infection, so I was placed on drugs and injections. After some time, I did not see my period again and I complained to my mum, who took me to another hospital again for scanning; and after that, they confirmed I was pregnant. That was where my ordeal started.

It was not funny when I realized that I was pregnant, especially with the thought of me betraying my parents. I felt so bad and of course I will never be happy, because it's out of wedlock. A lot of people criticized me, said awful things too about me, but what I comforted myself with was if God could allow this thing to happen, allow the pregnancy to be hidden from me and my parents, then he has a purpose for it. So I took it upon myself to close my ears from any other thing that I will hear. God was my comfort, my mum was there, my dad and siblings. So the thought in my heart was, I believed the child was going to be a great person; seeing him every day makes me happy.

My greatest motivation to keeping the baby was my mother her reaction. She was calm, encouraged me. I pray God will bless me someday to bless and make her happy. How do I feel now that I am a mother? Am proud of myself, am I happy I kept the baby? Unlike some in the process of aborting the child, either dead, or facing a lot of challenges, mine is different.

My advice to teenagers out there? Be careful, not everything that seems good from the outside is good. Just try and keep yourself, try and keep your dignity, don't allow someone to deceive you, it does not count, it's a lie. Your virginity is one of your most valued assets that once it's lost you can't get it back; but you live in regrets and insecurity about the action you take.

When I was growing up, I hoped to stay a virgin till I get married, I broke any relationship that made me break the promise.... until I met this guy who I got attracted to and eventually lost my virginity to, the painful part of is that's just that first time I had sex; and I got pregnant. So, I left for a French school in Niamey, which my dad paid a lot of money for, and I had to drop out when I realized that I was pregnant.

Hmm...I felt my world falling apart or rather coming to an end... I thought of how this was going to affect my dad's reputation and how my parents will feel/react. I thought of how people were going to look at me not knowing it was my first time, I cried and prayed to God to do a miracle and make the pregnancy disappear...

My parents were disappointed in me, my mum cried, my dad said nothing but I could feel his pain... People mocked me saying "hmm missionary's kid, let's see how they'll handle it"; people said disrespectful things; but I kept silent, even when they said it to my face, I just took it and went my way. Definitely I feel bad but what could I say when I gave them a reason to look down on me?

All I thought of was the future, I knew I had a bright future, so whatever I do today affects my tomorrow... I always told myself these people criticizing me today will see me prosper and I prayed to God to keep them alive for me. No one is above mistakes yeah?

I couldn't terminate the pregnancy because deep down within me I knew it was wrong, I was also scared but what actually motivated me to keep the pregnancy was my Aunt and her husband, they've been married for many years without a child and she told me with tears in her eyes, Sara let me not hear that you terminated this pregnancy.... that was when I had a second thought.

From the first day I set my eyes on my child, I felt this joy, everything bad people said about me never mattered any more, I read books that healed me; no more regrets, all I wanted was to make it in life to give my boy what he deserved and also make my parents proud.

Most times, when teenagers are faced with this challenge, they tend to get scared and only a few choose to have their babies. There are different emotions that come to mind;

Firstly, Denial, which always feels like a dream too bad to be true,

Secondly, Fear, fear of what her parent's response will be, what other people will think about her, and especially her boyfriend, what his reaction will be and

Thirdly, Guilt and Shame, feeling rejected, like an abandoned person, with these emotions and thoughts, most girls are likely to go for the option of abortion at that point.

It is difficult to stop abortions, because different countries have different legislations towards that, but you can do your best to protect your child first by ensuring she has the right company thereby avoiding pregnancy and then ensuring that abortion cannot be an option in the position where the child finally falls victim.

Adolescents who may want to avoid pregnancies may not be able to do so due to knowledge gaps and misconceptions on where to obtain contraceptive methods and how to use them. Adolescents face barriers to accessing contraception including restrictive laws and policies regarding provision of contraceptive, based on age or marital status, health worker bias and/or lack of willingness to acknowledge adolescents' sexual health needs, and adolescents' own inability to access contraceptives because of knowledge, transportation, and financial constraints. Additionally, adolescents may lack the agency or autonomy to ensure the correct and consistent use of a contraceptive method. At least 10 million unintended pregnancies occur each year among adolescent girls aged 15-19 years in developing regions.

An additional cause of unintended pregnancy is sexual violence, which is widespread with more than a third of girls in some countries reporting that their first sexual encounter was coerced.

A girl can conceive from sexual intercourse as early as she starts to ovulate. Usually, the first ovulation takes place after the first menstrual bleeding, the menarche. Girls experience menarche at very different ages and it is quite difficult to estimate the mean age at menarche worldwide, because significant differences between individual countries, but also between subpopulations within a country, are observable. Commonly, the mean age at menarche is considered as 13 years, the median, however, as 14 years. Consequently, today menarche occurs mainly in the first half of the second decade of life. From the viewpoint of human life history theory, this stage of life is called adolescence: Adolescence starts with pubertal hormonal changes such as the activation of the hypothalamus-pituitary-gonad-axis and can be divided into early and late adolescence. Early adolescence is defined as an age of 15 years and below, late adolescence means an age of 16–19 years. From the viewpoint of evolutionary biology, adolescence seems to be a very recent phenomenon. It is not found before *Homo sapiens* and may lead to a fitness advantage because it is a phase of socio-sexual maturation and of acquisition of social and economic skills which may increase reproductive success during later life. During early adolescence, successful reproduction was and is rare.

The years following menarche are often characterized by anovulation and consequently the likelihood of successful conception is quite low. Furthermore, a mean age of menarche of 13 years is a quite recent phenomenon. Although the reliability of data concerning age at menarche in historical times has to be questioned, it can be assumed that over the past 180 years the age of menarche has fallen substantially across all developed countries. In the 1840s, the average age at menarche was 16.5 years in Europe; today, menarche onset occurs at the age of 12.5 on the average in Europe. This decline of menarche age is the consequence of the so-called secular acceleration trend, which was induced by improved living conditions, infection control, and an improvement of nutrition. In the 1990s, the secular trend in menarcheal age had slowed down or ended in many European countries and the United States.

Better living conditions and sufficient food supply, however, resulted not only in earlier sexual maturation but also in an increase in the rate of ovulatory cycles soon after menarche. In other words, the risk of becoming pregnant shortly after menarche increased too. The secular trend, however, affected not only sexual maturation, on the other hand peak height velocity and the development of secondary sexual characteristics such as breast development take place much earlier and most adolescent girls often look like young ladies, long before they reach mental maturity.

Consequently, these girls may feel that they are old enough to start with sexual activity. Although sexual freedom and activity patterns among adolescent girls differ markedly according to cultural and religious background, we have to be aware that today nearly half of the global population is less than 25 years old. Even the generation of adolescents, that is, individuals between 10 and 19 years, is the largest in our history. Worldwide, an increasing number of adolescents tend to develop increased interest in sexual activities and consequently we are faced with increasing rates of sexually transmitted diseases including human immunodeficiency virus/acquired immune deficiency syndrome (HIV/AIDS) but also of unintended pregnancies and all associated social and medical risks of early childbearing among adolescent girls.

Every person's story is different, some people struggle and some not as much. If anyone tells you it is easy being a mother or father they are 100% lying; if it's easy you're not doing it properly! Challenges face you every step of the way but you don't just cry about them you figure out how to deal with them, and just cope with whatever faces you each step of the way.

Your priorities change for the better most times, you cannot change the way your life went. Having a child so young was difficult because you have a lot of stereotypes to get judged by no matter what. So why not just make the right decision by you and your child. Try by all means to avoid falling pregnant so young obviously, but if it happens remember there is always help out there, and it is not the end of the world.

I'd say to young girls thinking about having sex; just think about it. Ask yourself, "If I do this then what will happen? Even if you don't get pregnant, different things can happen. Be careful about it. Be sure that it's what you want. If you are going to do it, talk to someone first, a nurse, a friend, someone older. As someone who is thinking of changing the world to become a better place, you are not even permitted to think of having sex at that age; only when you are happily married, then can you build a happy family.

Consequences of Teenage Pregnancy

Future

If such a situation happens, what becomes of the future of that girl? Her education is not determined, her chances of making it far as has always been her dream is shattered, she battles with a lot of thoughts on what to do and how to go about that; in some cases, the girl begins to think of what will become of her parents if she is from a notable home or background.

Early marriage

In such times, if the girl resides in the rural area or maybe her parents who are trying to ensure that they do their best in sponsoring her education (and that of her other siblings), the best decision is for her to live with the father of the child (most parents will not accept that she stays with them again); and if any of these cannot be adhered to, then abortion (which we will talk a bit about) always becomes the last option, most especially if the girl cannot open up with either her mother or father or any member of the family she is usually open to. In the case that she chooses the marriage, she is more likely to experience violence from the man/boy of what she is not socially ready for, because she is still under the developing and growing process.

Stigma/trauma

Pregnancy outside of marriage comes with a lot of trauma... facing her immediate community; most especially her parents who have always 'believed in her', other children in the community who have always looked up to her as a godly example to be emulated and perhaps peers who will now make her feel dejected, finding it difficult to move around the community comfortably; because something has changed about her, something is new and strange about her.

Health

Another hazard that cannot be looked down on pending the decision of parents, the boy, the girl and peer influence is the health aspect which concerns teenage pregnancy.

The victim mostly falls in the hands of unqualified doctors which end up complicating the issue in aborting the pregnancy, because it's illegal. Either she loses her womb, complications arise, fertility and loss of blood and in worst cases might lead to death. That's why some countries both in Africa and some other parts of the world have legalized abortion as a way to cope the menace of illegal abortion and termination. I am not and will never encourage that, this is because the scripture in its entirety is against murder, and once a girl commits abortion, she has murdered a child. And God does not like such inhumane acts. One other reason in abortion is the act keeps haunting her, leading to regrets, and fears of the unknown.

Lack of education

In most African homes, especially rural areas, that becomes the end of the girl's education; who will take care of both her and the child? Who will pay the fees of both mother and daughter? Who will do this and that? And before you know, the girl becomes a school drop-out, she now has to begin to do menial jobs at home to cater for herself, the expected child and the family, and most often farming and trading becomes the last resort. Now because of such factors she becomes a young mother with less educational background. In the urban areas, if the girl is lucky, she is sent back to school, so narrowly escapes the same peer of her mate in the rural area; but the difference is that she has been delayed for a year or two; and the pain is that her mates and peers are now ahead of her both in class and other disadvantages which she has to cope with.

So, if the victim is in high school, she might have to drop out of school; if in the tertiary she struggles with her studies and the trauma of being pregnant at that age. Most times, the girl is scared to inform or open up to her parents what really happened.

Since she is not educated to even think of going out to look for a job which will help her care for the needs of the child, she becomes dependent. Now dependency in this regard is in two ways, either to her parents or to the boy. So let me start with the home briefly and then the boy: Parents- in the home, instead of them to focus on taking care of her needs as a girl, they now have to go an extra mile because of the new child; so they provide for both mother and child as well as other siblings in the family, it really is burdensome for them. The boy – that is if he accepts the baby to be his, he now has to provide all the baby's needs and the girl's as well. Making life difficult both for him and for the girl and even the newborn child; because they are not just both young, but they learn parenting at a young age doing things that are not equal to their initial task as teenagers.

What's the way out?

If the family as a unit fails, then the whole society becomes victims of that failed system. Some girls are taken advantage of, and are usually forced to keep mum or threatened to avoid any harm upon them, and this might be done either by any family member who is superior to her, neighbour or even someone in the church or some trusted friends of the parents; it's quite devastating. And some of them who end up having successful abortion now find it a habit to keep engaging in such illicit activities leading to more abortions, because they are already abused so the feeling that nothing good can become of them now govern their thoughts.

Be bold

The scripture says – For God hath not given us the spirit of fear; but of power, and of love, and of a sound mind. 2 Timothy 1:7 (<u>King James Bible</u>). The fear of the unknown is one of the greatest fears that has taken over the thoughts of children in this century. What if I refuse to tangle? I don't want to lose my friends because they are the ones I grew up with and know well. What if he decides to break up with me and go for my best friend? How will I cope if I don't have a boy/girlfriend like my peers? I can't go there because I don't have company. But always remember it pays to stand out differently; amazing enough, all of those who are pressuring you as a teenager to be like them are equally envying your lifestyle. So the best way is to make you believe that nothing is special about you, but you need to stand your ground in what you believe in. Great people are not ordinary, they don't think and act ordinary, every step and decision they take is always mind blowing and calls for attention, that's who you are. But unless you are bold as a teen, the enemy will make you believe you can settle for anything and still succeed; but it's never true. When you are able to defeat fear as a teen, the you will now be empowered with power and sound mind to make choice/decisions that will make everyone confirm to it; you might start the journey alone, but believe me you will not end alone

Know your self-worth

Here comes the big question…who are you? The moment you can answer the question of who I am, then believe me you can walk any path in life and still be the same and come out a victor. That's the only question that will save you as a teen from been pregnant out of wedlock, that's the only question that will make you stand your ground and say no to any form of advances from the males' sex, the question that will make you stay focused even when everyone is doing it and it seems right in the eye and appealing to the flesh, the question that will make you know what responsibility you carry and why you have to stay on track and not be misled, the question that will make you fight any adult or rapist that tries to force his way through you until you become a victor, the question that will make you become a model because you pushed through against all odds until those who were laughing at you now either celebrate with you or regret that they never saw what the happy end result will be like. You are not just a teenager, you are a teen with a purpose, on a mission, with a vision and mind-set, to conquer and set new records, to be a representative and to be just that the best way you can. Joseph was also flesh and blood mind you, but he ran not because he could not have accepted her advances, he knew where he was headed for and cannot allow anyone and anything to come in-between. Now let me ask, was he laughed at? Was his end the same? What makes you think you will not face the same fate, and when you stand true, what makes you think you will not be celebrated? Dare to be different. In addressing this, I might be speaking to the children but through the parents; because you are in the proper position to let your children know this.

Take responsibility

Am not a parent, so might not be in the better position to talk here perhaps. It's quite understood when you get angry, shout, weep, feel disappointed, broken and how you will now be seen in the society by others, but you need to understand that a child is a child and you are his/her parents. When you are strict, your children will be loose and open to whatever force and pressure that comes their way, when you are too strict and overprotective, you equally scare them away from opening up to life's challenges they are facing, thereby endangering them when they finally have the chance to be out of your reach. You have to make them your friends, your best friends, sharing your worries, pains, troubles, failures, dreams and desires with them; making them know you care about their daily engagements; opening them to life's reality. They should know that someday they will not be with you, but you trust that all they have learnt from you, they will be able to use wisely. Make time to stay with them, play and engage with them; when you take these responsibilities, believe me it will be very difficult for your child to hide even that secret he/she has been keeping from everybody. Be it relationships, sex life and the rest; open them up to sex education and pregnancy, dangers of engaging in early relationships and the rest, it goes a long way saving you the stress and pain of crying when it's too late to quench the fire.

Engage them

For some years now, through God's help, myself and some friends have been running a program we tagged G.M.I (Great Minds Initiative); a programme where young people are being convened together with the purpose of building and raising them in God's standard and foundation. With the aim of Mentoring children and teens/youths to know God, realizing who they are in Christ and their individual purpose in life; Raising children, teens, and youths that will live godly lives and grow with the mind-set that hunger and thirsts for doing exploits for God; Giving every child/teen/youth the privilege and opportunity to show and actualize his/her gift/talent. And thanks to parents who have stood by us all these years in moving this programme forward, we've heard testimonies from participants who have told us what the programme has done to them and how they now see things differently. If you are busy, ensure they attend Christian programmes that will distract them from all forms of peers that will cause harm to their lives; and they should be accountable at the end of the programme to you and the organizers. By doing that, you know what kind of teens they will meet in such places, people who will make them rise to equally take responsibility and be focused as well.

Be rooted in the word

This Book of the Law shall not depart from your mouth, but you shall meditate on it day and night, so that you may be careful to do according to all that is written in it. For then you will make your way prosperous, and then you will have good success – Joshua 1:8 (<u>English Standard Version</u>)

So, as a parent, how well have you helped your child in knowing, practicing and living according to the pattern in the scripture? You cannot help your child beyond the level in which you have ascended in your spiritual growth; so this scripture drove it further in - When I was a child, I was speaking as a child, I was led as a child, I was thinking as a child, but when I became a man, I ceased these childish things – 1 Corinthians 13:11(Aramaic Bible in Plain English). So my pastor explained better, when you now become an adult, you think like an adult, lead as an adult and speak like an adult.

What your child faces in his time is not the same as what you faced in your day, and it will not be the same as what his/her children's generation will face, and I believe that you are already seeing some of those things. Once you teach or train your child in the pattern of the Scripture like the likes of Josiah, Jesus, your child cannot bring your head to the grave.

Self-esteem

This deals directly with the child, but there needs to be a trigger or motivation. While I was a student, I never liked talking, because I was afraid they would laugh at me when I say or call a word incorrectly. But that was almost the same time I recalled I embarked on reading books and going to the Library. Not long after that, I could speak openly, and that became the trend. Self-esteem is different from being talkative, trying to prove you can do better than others and so on; too much of high self-esteem is dangerous to a child's character, likewise low self-esteem. There needs to be a balance, and that will only be done when parents notice that and work on it to help the child not to be a victim of teenage pregnancy as a result of either trying to prove she is now matured or grown up, while the boy tries to prove he is equally man enough to have sex or trying to hide secrets there by leading to silence even when struggling with urge and desires. Self-esteem is what every child must learn to develop, to become a better version of him/herself.

At that age, you have a lot of peers/friends within the same age group. A girl getting pregnant at that age, now sees her peers and friends moving forward in education and other aspects of life, it brings or lowers down the girl's self-esteem. Because she now loses confidence in herself, not being able to stand amidst them, and the stigma it comes along with, it really affects a girl's self-esteem. Most especially, when parents are not helping to calm the tension, she is facing, always insulting, making life look unbearable, and at times insisting on her to marry the man/boy who might not be responsible enough to cater for himself, her needs and that of the child, all these leads the girl to feel so bad about herself, making her lose her confidence in herself and thoughts of nothing seems good about her. Self-esteem plays a major role, especially when the girl doesn't have a good support system, or when the people around her, or the man/boy is not understanding. And if she is not strong enough, it could lead to suicide or abortion.

Parents-Child communication

In most cases, it is the failure of parents that results in that; in such cases, parents must learn to accept their faults and take responsibility along with the girl to grow and raise an innocent future. Let the girl know who she is as a child of God and then her worth in the society at a young age, because when she grows knowing and believing that, she lives with the realization forever. And as a teenage girl, you need to be open to your parents, you will fight, argue, quarrel and disagree, but make sure either your mother or father is your best friend, amongst them, you should be able to confide in one of them.

So, if a child is pregnant, what is the way out for you as a parent? Neglecting the child, shouting and creating barriers of communication between you? Calling the child names and causing more pains and psychological trauma on that child? Or finding out positive solutions that will build and raise the hopes of that child, making her believe that even though the deed has been done; there is hope if the proper measures are taken. When your child is wrong, he or she does not want you to remind them, they want you to understand that they are humans like you who can also make mistakes; in such times you are in the better position to draw the child to your warm embrace and speak to the child as a parent should do. Remember words are life, most especially in such times; so your reaction depends on the next decision that the child takes. And if the girl has made up her mind to keep the child, believe me she is already a hero and should be separated, because she has just broken the jinx that abortion is the last resort.

For other solutions, if by chance she decides to keep the pregnancy, there are options she can choose from also:

1. **Parenting the child:** In this condition/situation, she will learn to make sacrifices, making her life take a new dimension and having to play a role with the father of the child to raise him/her; in the case that the father does not take responsibility of raising the child, she will have to take the role of parenting herself if she chooses to parent.

2. **Adoption:** She will have to consider how that will affect her life if she decides to let go of her child. More so, contacting a very good adopting agency which she has to put into consideration.

3. **Foster Care:** Which is similar to adoption but in this case temporary, i.e., keeping the child with a family or hers to look after before she makes her decision of parenting the child or not. This decision might be a result of financial difficulty she is facing, but she has had the thought of keeping the child.

ABORTION

If a girl is pregnant, who pushes for abortion? The Boy, Girl, Parents or Peer influence?

What then is Abortion?

Abortion is the ending of a <u>pregnancy</u> by removal or expulsion of an <u>embryo</u> or <u>foetus</u>. An abortion that occurs without intervention is known as a <u>miscarriage</u> or "spontaneous abortion" and occurs in approximately 30% to 50% of pregnancies. When deliberate steps are taken to end a pregnancy, it is called an <u>induced abortion</u>, or less frequently "induced miscarriage". The unmodified word abortion generally refers to an induced abortion.

Let's equally consider the story of "**brave victims**" who could open up to share the stories. In as much as they are wrong, blaming them is not the best option, because it takes someone who has really repented and wants another to take life carefully and avoid these circumstances to open up.

My name is anonymous, I was in love with this amazing brother who was my fiancé and we were engaged to be married. Our families were already acquainted and preparations for the formal introduction were on top gears. We had dated for three years and every day our love was always a new thing; we were never out of love. So, I was leaving for service and since we were engaged to be married, we felt it was okay to oblige our uncontrolled feelings of having sex as a way of consummating our love. It actually felt okay and I did not feel any guilt at first.

We had sex on April 26, 2019. My monthly flow was to come between 15th-18th May, but it never came. At first, I waved it as a change in my cycle but my unusual constant irritating and unnecessary nagging and getting offended by any little thing got me thinking it's something else. I began to eat more than usual. It was at this point that I began to pray fervently to God to make my suspicions wrong. I began to make promises I knew I was not going to fulfill to God as long as my suspicions would be wrong. I summoned courage and told my fiancé about my suspicions. His calm reaction about my suspicions was very uncanny. He told me to go for a blood test and be sure whether I was pregnant or not. Going for a blood test in a laboratory was something I was very unwilling to do. My personality was at stake. I summoned yet another courage and took myself to a laboratory very far from where I was staying. And I had a ring on my finger to make me look married and comfortable. Few minutes in that lab took forever for me. The suspense and anxiety was overwhelming. The innocent radiant smile on the nurse as she handed me my result in a white envelope only aided in shattering my heart. I immediately began to silently pray in my heart that someone walks in and says there was a mistake. But it did not happen oooo! This was not Nollywood; this was my reality. Immediately I was out of the laboratory, I boarded a tricycle and headed home. As I opened the neatly sealed envelope, my heart literally shattered. Seeing the boldly written "POSITIVE" beside the box marked for pregnancy only brought hot uncontrollable tears from my eyes. My head began to spin round and fast. A lot went through my mind.

My personality was at stake. I was a committed church girl. I was a strong member in the youth fellowship with a leadership position in the drama wing. I was a band member, a Girls' Brigade officer. I had leadership positions in fellowships outside my home church. I am the first born of my family and was meant to be a model for my younger ones. Mothers in church and my neighbourhood always cited me as an example to their daughters and some brought their daughters to me to mentor them. As a matter of fact, I always preached against premarital sex and anything related to sexual immortality. Another reason was my parents' image. My mother was the women leader in my church, my father a titled man and a very revered man in my family, church, and community. My fiancé was the band leader in his church, he was also a discipleship coordinator in his local church, his church has this rule of asking people who want to be baptized to bring names of people they wanted to be their spiritual parents, and his name was always submitted to be a spiritual father, so he was a spiritual mentor to many young ones in his church. I asked myself questions like: what will people say about me? How will those mothers who brought their daughters to me to mentor them feel??? My mother will be very heart broken and will be stripped off her leadership position in church. My father will be very disappointed to say the least. His integrity was at stake. Then there was my fiancé... do you know he sometimes gets invited as a minister in conventions, conferences, crusades, churches and interdenominational gatherings. Some of those gatherings I followed him to, I've seen people fall under the anointing as he ministers. Imagine the utter disappointment and the huge disgrace that would befall him if people found out that he was a fornicator. I on the other hand was at the verge of getting excommunicated from partaking at the Lord's table.

I called my fiancé and told him the test was negative. You might want to ask why I lied to him about it??? My reason was simple.... when we started dating, we agreed on no sex until marriage and we never indulged in kissing on the lips or anything that would tempt us to fall. The highest form of showing affection in our relationship was holding hand, cooking, cleaning and singing together and we seldom hugged but he always kissed me on the forehead; he really adored me. Why should he then fall this greatly? He loved children very much and he prayed for the day he would behold his own. I felt this was not the answer to his prayers. I felt his ministerial career will face enormous disgrace. I can't allow him to fall like that; after all it was my fault; I was careless and it should not affect him. He worked hard to build a good image for himself and I was not going to destroy that image for him. Another reason was, we had a little quarrel before I found out I was pregnant and our relationship was really going rough at that time. We were always arguing and disagreeing on irrelevant issues, we went days without chatting, not talking on calls to the point that my friends noticed how my phone became unusually less busy. So, I felt telling him I was pregnant for sure will make him feel coerced into being with me. You might want to ask why I felt so; it's because his attitude towards me changed. He changed from that man I saw as my answered prayer to a familiar stranger. His temper was always high, his love for me became very cold and I feared a transfer of aggression to my unborn child. So, I made up my mind not to tell him I was pregnant.

The idea of aborting my child never crossed my mind. I had decided to have my baby by myself since I was far away in a strange man's land. I told myself I was not going to come back home after my POP. I concluded I was going to give birth and wait until my baby was at least 3 months old after delivery before I came back home. I had a side job already so sustaining me was settled. I felt with a child, I will boldly face any ridicule that came my way. As for my parents, seeing their first grandchild will soften their hearts. I will just tell them that a man from where I served is the father of my baby and I lost his contact after I found out I was pregnant. That was a perfect plan for me and I was going to take it to the next stage.

After two weeks from discovering I was pregnant, I began to fall ill; I was vomiting everything I ate, my waist was aching me like I was being hit with nails, I ran a temperature and my body felt like I was being cooked. I became a walking dead; the pregnancy was dealing with me to the point I felt that was my punishment from God for fornicating. So, while struggling with those pains, I overheard some ladies talking about abortion and a doctor who was a professional at it. Unfortunately for me, one of the ladies there asked critical questions like his name, where he hails from, his number, his address and at a point, we felt she wanted his services but she was just asking because she had a hunch that her boyfriend was the doctor. Unknowingly to them, I had taken that information about the doctor on my phone. And why I did that I could not say. A week passed and my health grew worse to the point that my P.P.A (Primary Place of Assignment) gave me 2 weeks break to treat myself. So, one day as I was going through notes on my phone, I stumbled on the doctor's information. I convinced myself to call him. I called him and he told me he charges ₦15000 for a month-old pregnancy and the money doubles as the pregnancy advances. I was two months gone already so if I needed his services, I was to pay ₦30000. I told him I would get back to him. Unfortunately for me, he kept calling to ask what my decision was and my health was not getting better. That was when I made up my mind to foolishly and selfishly abort my God given gift to me. It was one of those Salah holidays and I journeyed from where I was serving to Calabar. I left for Calabar as early as 7am and arrived in Calabar by 1 pm. I waited for the doctor in his house because he had patients in the hospital he needed to attend to. I found out that he did not do the abortion services in the hospital because it was illegal to do abortion in that state. He came back around 5pm and we proceeded to kill my unborn baby. He gave me anaesthesia to make me feel numb so that I won't feel the pain. Before he gave me the anaesthetic, he explained to me the implications: he can carry out the abortion without giving me the anaesthetics if I can bear the pains. Bearing the pains means I will not move no matter the pains else I risk serious injuries that would lead to me losing my womb. The anaesthetic will make me temporarily paralyzed and unable to feel anything but it will take long before it expires and I get back myself. So since it was 5pm already, he asked if I had plans to spend the night. I had no plans of spending the night so I said no but insisted on him giving me the anaesthetic. It was painful enough that I had the mind to kill my child but to be conscious while the act was ongoing was gruesomely selfish.

When I finally woke up by 7pm, all I could remember was taking an anaesthetic injection. I was lifeless and could not move. The room was spinning round and everything was blurry. I tried to move but the doctor advised me to relax first; the anaesthetics was still active in me. By 8pm, I was able to move and could see clearly. I paid him ₦30,000 and left his house. It began to rain but I was determined to go home. I boarded a bike to the junction and as I alighted, I was lucky enough to get a lift from Calabar to the next state. I was drenched already and my teeth were shaking. I was literally shaking. Luckily for me, the car that offered me a lift was going to my destination; he had a friend's payment of dowry. He asked what was taking me to Enugu this late and I said I stayed there. He asked what brought me to Calabar and I told him I came for a burial. Innocently, he sympathized with me. He noticed I was shivering so he switched on his car heater to make me feel warm. This man went as far as buying me hot goat meat pepper soup with coffee to push it down. He was really kind to me. We arrived in Enugu at careless minutes past 1am. We stayed at different locations but he was kind enough to take me to my house before going to his own house.

For me, I was not compelled by anyone to abort my child; it was solely my decision looking at the shame and disappointment I will bring on everyone. Since that abortion in July, there was never a day I went to sleep without shedding painful tears. After the abortion, I felt like I was smelling. I became disgusted at the sight of me. I hated myself. I was gradually falling into depression until one of my spiritual father's reached out to me. He counselled me, prayed for me and gave me communion after I told him everything. He admonished me to go on intense spiritual exercise. I prayed, fasted, studied the word and my prayer point was simple... MERCY... all I prayed for was God's MERCY and for the devil to flee with his condemnation that was creeping slowly and making me feel God was and will never be interested in me. My regrets were and will still remain about killing my unborn baby.

My advice on premarital sex is... resist the devil and he will flee away from you. Resisting means no kissing, caressing, smooching, dirty and nasty talks about sex, no pornography and most importantly, don't be idle for you never can tell what breeds in an idle mind. The mind needs renewal and it can only get renewed in the word, intense study. And only by constant renewal of the mind can one be able to stand firm to rules like no sex until marriage. Because we wrestle not against flesh and blood but against principalities and powers.

Once you get pregnant out of wedlock, you get reasons to abort and after you abort the child, you realize you actually had millions of reasons to have kept the child. The regret is much more than the shame you would ever face in this life. The word of God is true and a child whether born in or out of wedlock still remains a blessing. Abortion should never cross our minds, because we have no right over life that we can't give. I made a mistake and I regret my actions, and I will never go back to it. I had the chance to live by grace, you might not have the chance like me, so don't test God and don't take his grace for granted.

Another question we might have to ask, is what leads to abortion? The girl is discouraged? No one to give her right counsel, or maybe she refused to open up on her status as at the time she finds out she is pregnant, the strictness/harshness of parents towards handling issues that pertains to their children's life? I've heard cases whereby a mother pushed for the abortion, because she is the head of a unit in the church or a respected person, and to her understanding, if that child is kept what will become her reputation in the church, before her peers, where she worked and the rest. The guy now begins to think of himself becoming a father at an early age, how will he foot the bills of both the mother and the child, how can he move around his peers without people making reference to him, and other thoughts; while the girl faces more of the problem, both psychologically, socially etc.

Around 56 million abortions are performed each year in the world, with about 45% done unsafely. Abortion rates changed little between 2003 and 2008, before which they decreased for at least two decades as access to family planning and birth control increased. As of 2018, 37% of the world's women had access to legal abortions without limits as to reason. Countries that permit abortions have different limits on how late in pregnancy abortion is allowed.

Historically, abortions have been attempted using herbal medicines, sharp tools, forceful massage, or through other traditional methods. Abortion laws and cultural or religious views of abortions are different around the world. In some areas abortion is legal only in specific cases such as rape, problems with the foetus, poverty, risk to a woman's health, or incest. There is debate over the moral, ethical, and legal issues of abortion. Those who oppose abortion often argue that an embryo or foetus is a human with a right to life, and they may compare abortion to murder. Those who support the legality of abortion often hold that it is part of a woman's right to make decisions about her own body. Others favour legal and accessible abortion as a public health measure.

Some Parts of the world have made abortion legal, with the aim to reduce death rate in the youths through illegal means of abortion, and families/societies who have family planning and mistakenly the woman took in, so they have to use this procedure and other means. It is almost impossible to stop the spread of abortion in the society, but you cannot deny its effect to both the victim(s) and the society. Looking at the African culture and tradition most countries have refused to legalize abortion because it will rather cause more hazard to the young ages. With that being said, let us look at why abortion seems impossible to be legalized:

1- African Society's Love for Children

It is popularly known, and almost taken for granted, that in traditional Africa, even before the coming of Christianity, children were highly valued in society. This does not mean that there were no situations of abuse; there were cases where children were mistreated and neglected. The worst is in reference to the birth of twins. "The birth of twins and triplets is an event out of the ordinary. Therefore, in many African societies twins and triplets are treated with fear or special care. Formerly, some societies used to kill such children; others killed both the mother and the children. This, however, was not the universal practice, for other societies greeted the birth of twins with great joy and satisfaction, as a sign of rich fertility." All in all, the fact is that children were, and are still, seen as precious.

2- Marriage and Procreation

We must note that marriage and procreation in African communities are a unity: without procreation marriage is incomplete. ((MBITI, J. S., *African Religions and Philosophy*, p. 133). Pregnancy is the first indication that a new member is on the way. The expectant mother becomes, therefore, a special person and receives special treatment from her neighbours and relatives. This special treatment starts before and continues after child-birth. In some African societies, marriage is not fully consummated until the wife has given birth. For this reason, there is general abhorrence of barrenness in most African societies. "Unhappy is the woman who fails to get children for, whatever other qualities she might possess, her failure to bear children is worse than committing genocide: she has become the dead end of human life, not only for the genealogical line but also for herself".

3- Children as Survival of Race and Assurance of Personal Immortality.

As we indicated above, a woman who has not given birth to a child, dies in the eyes of African society; there will be nobody of her own immediate blood to 'remember' her, to keep her in the state of personal immortality: she will simply be 'forgotten'. (MBITI, J. S., *African Religions and Philosophy*, p. 110). Therefore, a child not only continues the physical line of life, in some societies thought to be a re-incarnation of the departed, but becomes the intensely religious focus of keeping the parents in their state of personal immortality. (MBITI, J. S., *African Religions and Philosophy*, p. 120) A person who, therefore, has no descendants in effect quenches the fire of life, and becomes forever dead since his line of physical continuation is blocked if he does not get married and bear children. This is a sacred understanding and obligation which must neither be abused nor despised. (MBITI, J. S., *African Religions and Philosophy*, p. 133).

4- Polygamy as Search for Children

Getting married to two or more wives is a custom found all over Africa, though in some societies it is less common than in others. The custom fits well into the social structure of traditional life, and into the thinking of the people, serving many useful purposes, one of which is the search for children. If the philosophical or theological attitude towards marriage and procreation is that these are an aid towards the partial recapture or attainment of the lost immortality, the more wives a man has the more children he is likely to have, and the more children the stronger the power of 'immortality' in the family. He who has many descendants has the strongest possible manifestation of 'immortality', he is 'reborn' in the multitude of his descendants, and there are many who 'remember' him after he has died physically and entered his 'personal immortality'. Such a man has the attitude that 'the more *we are*, the bigger *I am*'. Children are the glory of marriage, and the more there are of them the greater the glory. (MBITI, J. S., *African Religions and Philosophy*, p. 142, cfr. p. 98)

5-Communal Responsibility over Children's Well-being.

The birth of a child is, moreover, the concern not only of the parents but of many relatives, including the living and the departed. For it is the community which must protect the child, feed it, bring it up, educate it, and in many other ways incorporate it into the wider community. The child cannot be exclusively 'my child' but only 'our child'. "Children are the buds of society, and every birth is the arrival of 'spring' when life shoots out and the community thrives," writes Professor John S. Mbiti (MBITI, J. S., *African Religions and Philosophy*, p.110; see also MAGESA, L., *African Religion: the Moral Traditions of Abundant Life*, p. 83). In this kind of set-up, there are no children left abandoned. Even those children born out of wedlock, have a place in society; many families are willing to welcome such children and look after them.

6-The Mystique of Life, and Harmony in African Religion

The foundation and purpose of the ethical perspective of African Religion is life, life in its fullness. Everything is perceived with reference to this. It is no wonder, then, Africans quickly draw ethical conclusions about thoughts, words, and actions of human beings, or even of "natural" cosmological events, by asking questions such as: Does the particular happening promote life? If so, it is good, just, ethical, desirable, divine. Or does it diminish life in any way? Then it is wrong, bad, unethical, unjust, detestable. This most basic understanding of morality in African Religion or tradition is incorporated systematically in people's way of life. It is expressed in their traditions, ceremonies, and rituals. It constitutes what Africans perceive as the mystique of life. (MAGESA, L., *African Religion: The Moral Traditions of Abundant Life*, p. 77).

Similarly, for Africans, harmony as the principle for moral order does not mean that people and other members of creation lose their freedom. Harmony is *the* agent of freedom and is meant to enhance it. But what does "freedom" mean? Does it imply license or liberty to do whatever one wants? Such is not the case. In African Religion or tradition, freedom is what enables a person to be fully who he or she is. This applies equally to all beings: harmony enables a tree to be fully a tree, a stone fully a stone, and a person fully human. (MAGESA, L., *African Religion: The Moral Traditions of Abundant Life*, p. 74).

I can still remember one of the agreements and vows we took with a friend, we said we want to be the closest person our children should have in their lives, that when they are pregnant or have sex, they can confide in us not to break the trust, but to tell them what to do and how to go about it. If parents push for abortion based on their position either in church or the society, then they have ruined the life of that child; because such a child now sees that as a legitimate thing to do; because it was encouraged at home. It is risky, it is traumatic, especially when you know you did not raise the children in that manner which she lived; but it is the best decision you can take as a parent, that will save the child from all forms of psychological trauma, because once the home is behind them, they believe they can go through; but once the home is against such a child, any decision can make sense. So, am I encouraging abortion? NO. Am I saying it is bad for parents to feel bad and react the way they do? Absolutely No as well; but what I am emphasizing here is the deed has been done, the child is yours and you still have what it takes for you to turn the negative course of times to the positive, by that one reaction you will take i.e., standing by that child to the end.

Why Abortion?

Fear of the Unknown

Some of the girls don't want it to be said they gave birth in their parents' house out of wedlock, responsible men will not consider them when they hear they gave birth at home, why should they become a mother at a young age? They fear they will lose their fiancé and the trust of their immediate family as well people who once had hopes on them, and the exemplary life they have set overtime will diminish etc.

Some children think of abortion because they don't want to lose the trust of their parents, they don't want to hurt their feeling leading to shame rather than the pride they always have on them and as well the immediate society.

Lack of parental care

Parents, when you don't show your child the required care needed at home, do not expect such a child to keep that pregnancy; the thought of how the home will be alone can make her consider that option. When a parent is strict, he/she makes that child to be distant from him/her; when you don't trust them and show them love as at when needed, there is no way you will expect them to open their secrets to you, talk more of you giving them the option of keeping the child. One mother shared how she had to threaten her daughter from committing the act; first she sinned against God and secondly, she wants to commit abortion? The mother was against it, even though it was not her fault but due to the situation she had to leave the house. Upon discovering the daughter was pregnant, she had to insist she keep the pregnancy and now she is a happy grandmother of two children out of wedlock amongst many; her pride was that her daughter did not commit the act.

Personal

The reasons why women have abortions are diverse and vary across the world. Some of the reasons may include an inability to afford a child, <u>domestic violence</u>, lack of support, feeling they are too young, and the wish to complete education or advance a career. Additional reasons include not being willing to raise a child conceived as a result of rape or <u>incest</u>.

Societal

Some abortions are undergone as the result of societal pressures. These might include the preference for children of a specific sex or race, disapproval of single or early motherhood, stigmatization of people with disabilities, insufficient economic support for families, lack of access to or rejection of contraceptive methods, or efforts toward <u>population control</u>. These factors can sometimes result in compulsory abortion or <u>sex-selective abortion</u>.

Abortion happens mostly because either the girl, parents, fiancé finds it difficult to keep the pregnancy. When she decides to abort, she encounters a lot of problems- feelings of guilt, abortion looks like a quick fix at that time, feeling that the baby is just a tiny destiny filled human God is shaping, and that life matters a lot. The choice of abortion is most likely going to lead to complications, like heavy bleeding, chances of the inability to not bear children again; it also comes with a range of negative emotions like: guilt, regrets, anger, flash backs and night mares, can lead to withdrawal from people and other smaller kids around.

Abortion seems like a simpler solution, but it's not worth it. So, in case you are a girl, faced with this, it's better to keep the child, and even if it's so hard to fend for the baby, it's advised you give it for adoption.

Influence

The fact that you have influence over someone gives you the opportunity to insist that certain things be done right. Parents' influence in these trying times over their daughter is very crucial; at that point, the girl might not really know what step/decision to take and will solely depend on what option you feel is best for her. The moment there is the mention of abortion, she might be afraid at first, but she now thinks that might be the option since its suggested by you. That's the time you must forget what the immediate community looks like, the shame and other negative thoughts that will arise and think of the life of your child and the unborn child who is about to be innocently taken.

For the boy or fiancé, if you are afraid of being a father at a young age or your reputation, then you should not think of sex in the first place. She equally might look to you for options when she confides in you before her parents, with you in the picture of what happened between you both; thinking of abortion at that time might save you but might endanger her, her future and yours too. Also, know that you have less to suffer in times of shame or other forms of public disgrace like her, and your insistence might not be the best option but ensuring that she takes the right decision is important, which is to keep the baby. Instead of threatening her to flush the child out or you break up with her, why not think of other options for her own good and that of the child? Life was actually meant to be easy, but we made it become complex with our own hands.

Also, to the girl who is in the middle of all the dilemma, this is a situation between life and death and you are asked to choose; have you ever wondered if you were asked to take your life? Your response will never be yes, that's the situation here, between you and the unborn child you are carrying. You really need to shut your ears to any option that discourages you from keeping the child; yes, you might think of what the society will think and say about you; but the choice of keeping might be an opening, I am not saying this as a way of wooing you to keep the child actually, but you cannot tell what the child's existence might actually bring your way. See the future and think of it, rather than the present situation/circumstances, it might always look difficult at first, but might be the best; you will later be proud you refused to listen to whoever. It is your life, it is your body, so no one should choose for you to take your child, but you can also choose to keep the child.

What's The Way Out?

Early Sex Education

Most parents, especially Africans, find it very difficult to talk about sex with their children most especially the girls. They see it as something corrupt that will go and distort the thought pattern of the child, thereby causing harm to the child, but unknown to them that's what the child needs. As a parent, God has given you the wisdom and understanding on how to talk about sex education that will not be offensive but rather educative; all you do in such moment is you create awareness for your child at that early age, and that's where you tell her about her periods, danger of sex at an early stage/age, abortion, no sex before marriage and the likes that can be helpful to her as a teen. But when you shy away from that responsibility, believe me the child will surely want to know about those things that the parents are either scolding him/her for or refusing to talk to them about. That's why when they mingle/associate with their peers, they hear such foul and offensive words and statements. Coming back, they either ask you questions, or they now ask themselves questions that they need answers for, and who will provide the answer if not you? Failure to do so, out of their inquisitive nature, they end up in this mess; so open them up to it, but in a proper manner and time.

Orientation and campaigns

I will not advice that married people should be encouraged to have abortion, because children are gifts from God, but in cases of illness which makes it difficult for her to deliver and abortion becomes the only option available, one cannot deny that it should take place to save the wife than losing them both.

So, government agencies must also educate the young populace in the society and communities on dangers of indulging in abortion. And having strict policy in place to help cope with its effect, most times it leads to loss of both the girl/woman and the innocent unborn child.

At times, I think some of these girls/ladies are actually innocent, but due to pressure and trying to please others so as not to get hurt in the process, they end up getting involved in this menace. So a campaign must be introduced on NO SEX before marriage; and if such might not be adhered to, then the use of condom should be encouraged, so as to avoid pregnancy which can lead to abortion.

Knowledge of the word of God

Firstly, if you are a parent and encourage abortion due to your position and integrity, then the fear of God is not actually in you. If you are a Christian brother who found yourself in this mess and decide or allow your girl to be involved in abortion, you are not worthy to be called a Christian and to the girl, if you are also a Christian and engage in this act, then you are actually wicked; because you took a life knowing that God hates murder and will never encourage that.

Most times, what we call accidents in life were not actually accidents, and unless we see it from the same perspective God does and decide to accept it that way, we cannot fathom God's ways. Rahab was a Prostitute who became mother of generations, she was despised but is celebrated today, Mary, Lazarus' sister who poured perfume on Jesus' feet, the

Samaritan woman who brought salvation to the Samaritan community after she met Jesus at the well? All these were seen as disgusting, but the people could not deny that they are heroes. So what if God had allowed your child or fiancé to take in? I drew our minds to these so we know that in God's plan, nothing was ever a mistake, but the devil had to make us see it that way to deny us what God has in mind.

But with the presence of the word of God which is deposited in you as a father and mother, fiancé and the girl in the picture, there is always a God speaking, telling you what he wants you to do; and has promised to walk the path of disgrace, shame, fear of the unknown with you. What people will say and think and all the negative thoughts the devil puts in your mind are distractions. All you have to do is LOOK BEYOND the PREGNANCY and ABORTION and SEE THE BIGGER PICTURE.

Abortion indeed is not the best option, but victims are not to always to be blamed like those who shared their story. But thank God for their lives now, they have seen a bigger light the enemy did not allow them see and regrets of not keeping the child and why they should have kept it. Rather, the show of love and care can be of great help to those victims. My hope is for a day that a campaign will be put in place with victims who will be bold enough beyond just sharing their stories in written forms like this to sharing it publicly; so that someone who might be thinking of it or about being involved in the act, can take a stand and say, 'I cannot, I want to keep the baby for the bigger picture'. Everyone is afraid of what the society will say or think, but no one is afraid of what the unseen God is capable of.

Chapter 11

How About Peer Pressure/ Influence?

As humans, we all go through developmental phases. And as a Parent, you are one of the biggest influences on your teen. It may seem like they aren't listening, but they truly are. When parents stay involved in their children's lives, their kids tend to make better choices for themselves. As a teenager, your child's task is to take a break from you and your influence, and develop a separate sense of self. Part of this process is going from identifying with parents and their values and identifying with other peers' values. Friends become of utmost importance, and fitting in with a group of friends is a crucial task during this developmental stage.

One faithful evening, I decided to take a stroll down my area; one of the programmes we've been running was in the school i.e., G.M. I (Great Minds Initiative) where we commissioned the ONE BIG FAMILY Campaign, in which we engage schools, taking time with both Staff and Students of the School. I've been procrastinating on my visit to the house. So, on this day, I was bored at home, I decided to visit a house since it's not far from mine and know how they were faring; on reaching the compound, there were these other girls in the same compound who lived there, I have met them severally after school while coming back home and had this special attention to them, though never bothered to know where they stay or who their parents were and where they stayed; but most times after school we meet and we exchange pleasantries, but most especially the love between the eldest and her other siblings was amazing. So, I was surprised seeing them there and knowing it was not them I came to see, but then I was actually mistaking them for those other girls whom we've been running the programme with in their school. So, we greeted each other and I entered the house, normally what I do when visiting, I observe first the parents, children and the setting in which these children are being raised, behaviour at home compared to school, composure.

And when their mother came in, I was shocked to find out I knew the mum and the dad as well, since we are in the same area and have participated in some community works with him, but didn't know they were his children; we did not talk at length with the mum, but we exchanged pleasantries with her, and the reception was nice. So, I concluded that really there is not much difference between who they were outside and at home, even though I did not ask the parents, but you can tell when you see it too. Because there is a way a child behaves at home, that you can tell from who he is inside the house/home, his/her attitude wise and the rest. I was happy seeing that, and I encouraged them in what they need to do during the lockdown and pandemic period, what they need to do so as not to stay idle and what idleness could cause; so after our short but meaningful discussion, I decided to now go to the apartment of the initial girls I came to see/visit; surprisingly, I left an apartment that the children were different compared to whom these ones were in school. I was amazed, though they claimed two of their friends were celebrating their birthdays, all of them I've known since they were in the same school; so, I said, okay can you take me to your room? But I was surprised at their attitude, so I had to stay there waiting for the time they will lead me to their living room. I waited while they took their snapshots.

I was getting upset, but had to calm myself, so that at least I won't spoil the moment for the friends and give them a wrong impression, and after all I went to see them not that I was invited. So, I waited, after about five minutes of waiting the other twin decided to lead me to the living room. I saw the mum and I greeted her too since I knew her and I went inside and sat, at the time I was playing a game, so I sat and continued from where I stopped. I began observing like the previous one and my first observation was that the mother was preparing for the weekend while these "grown up girls' 'were on the other side of the house taking snapshots. I don't mind the treatment they gave me, but I was expecting to see and meet children or teens with the same character as I always see in school, but I concluded that it may be their agreement with the mum since the other one claimed she was up much earlier that morning to begin work in the house. So, I kept playing my game, and they would come in and go out as if I was not noticed, so I sat there and was taking my observation the best way, I felt I had to. The mum was still working; she was very busy while the girls were still with their friends. Later on, they all came inside and began to interact, I was served food which I declined, because I had told myself I am not eating anything there earlier on before the visit that evening. Surprisingly, the older one came and began to eat the food I was served and even said "maybe you are shy, so let me help you eat the food then", so I obliged, but the girl who brought the food was not happy, but I did not bother, because my mission was to visit and know how they were faring. And the girls began to lament of what her mum did, "My elder brother sent me ₦13,000 for my birthday, and my mum said she was using ₦10,000, not borrowing, and giving me just ₦3,000", and the other ladies were not happy with the mum's decision; and then the other girl whom I went to see now told them of a birthday party their mum had consented for them to organize in the house. But the older one was now showing them the picture of someone she claimed to be her guy, but called him her partner. I sat there, I did not join the conversation; and the girl said to me "you don't have to be shy, at least there is nothing to be shy, you know I will soon be a model so just feel free, good night".

Then I told myself, peer pressure, peer influence, who is to be blamed when the children associate with the wrong company? Parents, Children or Society? I was privileged to attend a school whereby my dad had to pay huge amounts of money, to ensure I finished there at all cost. I remembered times I really wanted to leave the school, due to pressure; no time to study, seniors trying to look for faults on you, to ensure you are at fault so they get you punished, and at times brutalize you; and we were able to survive that hardship and pressure. I've seen my seniors, being in the same room and dormitory with those who were drunkards, drug addicts and smokers; and then my SSS 3 was really a class of decision making, between exploring and mingling just to belong or be part. But I really cannot tell how I was able to scale through those behaviours and influences, though at a point I really wanted to have such experiences too, at that moment, you can just sit back and behave the way you feel like, either associating with the negative or positive side, either way you now have the freedom; but those were the moments I equally have to make the choice of not displeasing God, my parent and people who trusted and know me to be good. So, I changed, decided to pay the price by beginning to associate with people of like mind. I started working with children at a young age from 2010; knowing that I am working with children, I have to now consider what I have to permit them to learn. Those were some things that led me to go the opposite for good, and to avoid influences that will not help me pursue my goals and dreams.

Peer influence defines who a child is, what path he/she is likely to take, what norms and principles are to govern him/her. It is so serious that if parents, teens and youths as well as children and society don't take it seriously it ruins a child and person with a bright future.

If parents are able to do their homework well, of training and raising these children right, we would have less of the negative influence to the positive, but with the times we find ourselves in, it raises concern to the fact that there is a lot of work that needs to be done to cope and develop children and a society who will carry and raise with the positive mindset of influence.

Peer pressure, or influence, comes in several forms, and these types of peer pressure can have a tremendous impact on a young person's behaviour. Research shows the <u>most impressionable age for peer influence seems to be the middle school years</u>. This is when a child is forming new friendships and choosing an identity among those friends.

What is Peer Group/Influence?

Peer influence is when you **choose to do something** you wouldn't otherwise do, because you want to feel accepted and valued by your friends. It isn't just or always about doing something against your will.

You might hear the term 'peer pressure' used a lot. But peer influence is a better way to describe how teenagers' behaviour is shaped by wanting to feel they belong to a group of friends or peers.

Peers are people who are part of the same social group, so the term "peer pressure" means the influence that peers can have on each other. Although peer pressure does not necessarily have to be negative, the term "pressure" implies that the process influences people to do things that they may be resistant to, or might not otherwise choose to do.

So usually the term "peer pressure" is used when people are talking about behaviours that are not considered socially acceptable or desirable, such as experimentation with alcohol or drugs. The term "peer pressure" is not usually used to describe socially desirable behaviours, such as exercising or studying.

In reality, peer pressure can be either a positive or negative influence that one peer, or group of peers, has on another person.

Positive Peer Pressure

Peer pressure could influence a young person to become involved in sports. This involvement could be positive, leading to exposure to healthy lifestyles and role models, and eventually leading the young person to become a positive role model herself.

Negative Peer Pressure

That same peer pressure could lead the same young person to over-identify with sports, putting exercise and competition above all else. If taken to an extreme, she may develop exercise addiction, causing her to neglect schoolwork and social activities, and ultimately, use exercise and competition in sports as her main outlet for coping with the stresses of life. This can also lead to numerous health consequences.

Peer pressure causes a child to do things he/she would not otherwise do with the hope of fitting in or being noticed, and of course, this can include experimenting and adapting with the trending times they find themselves surrounded by.

Beyond prompting them to use drugs and other things that easily entangle, peer pressure or the desire to impress their peers can override a teen or tween's fear of taking risks, according to the National Institute on Drug Abuse for Kids. This risky behaviour can result in the following:

- Driving under the influence of substances or alcohol
- Overdose with illicit drugs and substances
- Alcohol or drug poisoning
- Asphyxiation
- Sexually transmitted diseases
- Accidents
- Addiction

For peer pressure to override a child to make him/her almost forget who he/she is, there must have been a little laxity from parents which was supposed to be a concern that has overtaken the child's mind-set and reasoning.

Although parents worry about the influence of peers, overall, parents also can have a stronger influence on whether children go on to develop addictive behaviours than peers do.

Addiction is a complex process, which is affected by many different factors, so peer pressure alone is unlikely to cause an addiction.

Rather than worrying about the effects of your children's friendships, parents would do well to focus on creating a positive, supportive home environment, free of addictive behaviours and without access to alcohol or other drugs. And at times, some of these influences start in the home, from the kinds of company your child associates with which the parents were unable to know or say anything about. Peer pressure is a powerful influence, one that you need to understand so that you can help protect your child from making harmful decisions done under its sway.

As humans, we all go through developmental phases. As an infant, your child needed to learn that you were trustworthy and would take care of all his needs. As a teenager, your child's task is to take a break from you and your influence and develop a separate sense of self. Part of this process is going from identifying with parents and their values and identifying with other peer's values. Friends become of utmost importance, and fitting in with a group of friends is a crucial task during this developmental stage.

Peer pressure/influence is a mind game, and once it gains control in the mind of your child, it can be negative or positive; it takes serious time for you to gain control over it again. That is why it is advised that in most cases, what you feed your child with from a young age determines the outcome when he grows/matures. So when you look at the society vividly, you will realize why negative peer pressure occupies more people's lives than positive and it is possible because of the negligence of parents to take control; but in another instance, it's not much of their fault, because, considering the geographical location the child is raised, you can tell what the possible outcome will be. A child who grew in an Urban area, Rural-Urban or Rural areas are all affected; from the Rural chances are high due to mix up or engaging with other peers from different background, Rural –Urban tries to fit into the company that he/she is comfortable with; while the Urban mostly mingle with children of those from the same class of the society. I will talk a bit about these 3 stages to help you understand how these 3 can either traumatize a child or develop him.

Rural Area: What are the common vices in those places? Teenage Pregnancy, Divorce, Drunkenness and Smoking, Sex and fornication, early marriages and so on. Living in those kinds of communities and being able to maintain a positive mindset is really difficult but possible because all of these vices mentioned are trending in such places; so it's either you associate with them or strive to make it through. This comes with ridiculing and the rest; but you know that you are doing the right thing and must have to strive, because what seems to be called ridicule will end up becoming celebrated.

Rural-Urban: In this kind of community or area, the children of the elite class always try to mingle with the children of the low…in most cases there is no positive influence, because they must have something in common that usually brings them together, most negative vises in these area include stealing, armed robbery, cultism, drinking and smoking, sex and partying, bullying and rape, abortion and high level of disregard to parents both at home and in the society, vulgar statement and use of pidgin as a language of communication and the rest. In this kind of community, it's a bit easier for a child to maintain a positive mindset, because you choose what company you want to associate with. May I also add a bit; the community or environment a child grows in/from really tells how he/she will live life in the later future. Community actually defines a child aside from the home/family, but it's the responsibility of parents to think of measures to put in place if they really want their child to carry and build on a positive mindset.

Urban Area: This community or settlement is mostly for the elite, so the children are the ones that have influence over each other; this one has higher chances of the children building and carrying a positive mindset to the others. This is because when the child comes or is raised from a family whose parents are strict about what kind of friends they keep, where they go and other issues that concern the child, he/she will hardly associate with those who have or carry the negative mindset. Negative cultures in these areas are: dressing culture, sex and partying, abortion, pride and arrogance, extravagant living, drinking and smoking, rape, care less about development and growth, clubbing, watching of pornography, gay and lesbian practices and so on. Parents in this area actually determine how the child is to be raised, either in the Godly way or not. This is because he/she can be limited to friends, and also the type of environment he/she lives in which causes less danger compared to the other two children raised in the others discussed.

So, who your child/teen calls a friend is very crucial for you as a parent, because as you are making efforts to raise your child in the right way, these influencers are equally making efforts as well; This is why your child's friends are so influential, they are "trying on" different thoughts, ideas, and lifestyles that these friends offer. It's not you—it's their destiny, developmentally speaking. But your major role in such a moment is to ensure they choose and associate with friends that will help them work towards fulfilling their purpose and not ruining it.

When your teenager's friends influence your child's thoughts or behaviour, that is <u>peer pressure</u>. This influence may be verbal, nonverbal or even unconscious on the part of your child's friends. This pressure can negatively or positively impact your teen's behaviour. Peer pressure is a powerful influence, one that you need to understand so that you can help protect your child from making harmful decisions done under its sway.

Like earlier mentioned, these are stages a child cannot run from and parents cannot deny or stop, but as parents you are supposed to play the major role in it; by ensuring you teach them what kind of friends to keep, engaging them in activities that will help them grow maturely at a young age, because when they reach that stage they are already thinking above that age, so they seem to have an edge over their peers, teaching them the word of God and its benefits as well as showing them examples of godly children both from the Bible and the larger society; letting them know of the expectations you have on them, and who you envision or want them to grow to become.

Other Kinds of Peer Pressure or influence asides the Positive and Negative are:

1. Spoken Peer Pressure: Spoken peer pressure is when a teenager asks, suggests, persuades or otherwise directs another to engage in a specific behaviour. If this is done in a one-on-one environment, the recipient of the influence has a stronger chance of adhering to his or her core values and beliefs. If, however, the spoken influence takes place within a group, the pressure to go along with the group is immense.

2. Unspoken Peer Pressure: With <u>unspoken peer pressure</u>, a teenager is exposed to the actions of one or more peers and is left to choose whether they want to follow along. This could take the form of fashion choices, personal interactions or 'joining' types of behaviour. Many young teens lack the mental maturity to control impulses and make wise long-term decisions. Because of this, many teens are more susceptible to influence from older or more popular friends.

3. Direct Peer Pressure: This type of peer pressure can be spoken or unspoken. Direct peer pressure is normally behaviour-centric. Examples of these kinds of behaviour would be when a teenager hands another teen an alcoholic drink, or makes a sexual advance, or looks at another student's paper during a test. The other teen is put in a position of having to make an on-the-spot decision.

4. Indirect Peer Pressure: Similar to unspoken peer pressure, indirect peer pressure is subtle but can still exert a strong influence on an impressionable young person. When a teen overhears a friend gossiping about another person and then reacts to the gossip, that is indirect peer pressure.

Very often, the drive to engage in this kind of behaviour is a result of peer pressure. Adolescents who have larger circles of friends appear to be less influenced by the suggestions or actions of their peers, but the pressure to conform is very real at this age.

What's the Way OUT??

Supporting healthy friendships

As mentioned earlier in one of the chapters, the best friend a child is supposed to have and relate with is the parents. The moment parents allow that gap to be created by allowing the child to associate with friends he/she becomes comfortable to communicate with, then it causes a big hazard. You can do this by staying connected to your child. This can help him feel more comfortable talking to you if he's feeling swayed to do something he's uncomfortable with. Most times, it's not in how strict or tough you are that makes the child adjust, you must know when it's time to discipline, love, play, pray, encourage your child as a parent. You have to learn these adjustments so as not to chase or send your child out of your arms into that of a company that will ruin your child and family reputation. Good communication and a positive relationship with your child might also encourage your child to talk to you if she's feeling negative influence from peers.

Modelling responsible behaviour

Have you imagined saying to your young teen or child, get ready, you are leading us tomorrow in the morning devotion? Or get ready, you are leading us in the sporting activities; you are the one to cook today while I will tell you what to do and at what times; you are going to water the flowers, weed the grasses in the surrounding. As little as these might seem to you as a parent, your child is already understanding and building a state of being responsible. The first time I cooked, it was awful, and that was years ago, but with the help of my mum I can cook as a woman/lady is supposed to cook. In other dishes that I have not learnt, she puts me through; now there is almost no dish I cannot cook. For a child to be responsible, parents must not think that it is when he grows, then he will know what he/she is supposed to do, be it cooking, reading the Bible, cleaning the house, respecting the elderly and parents, saying no to whatever entangles and will lead them astray all have to start from when the child is growing and beginning to learn. The early stage of learning is what will save you from regretting, being sad and talking about how other parent's children have grown to become responsible rather than yours. That's the discipline Proverbs talked about in the Bible, you missed it at the young age of the child, then you face the consequence of your action and negligence. Like the popular saying "a stitch in time saves nine", start the process now, irrespective of how emotional you can be at times, and appreciate the process, development and growth of who that child has turned out to be.

Keeping an open, judgment-free family dialogue

Keep communication lines open and search for signs that show their behaviour is changing, such as suddenly withdrawing, a change in clothing or rude language or behaviour. You must learn to trust your child; it is really very important. Know at what moment to engage him/her; when he or she has erred you, it pays a lot and builds stronger dialogue. Don't compare your child with another, it demoralizes that child, and leads to low self-esteem in most cases. Rather, give that expectation of who you want him/her to be, and encourage them to become that; by doing that, it becomes difficult for your child to be easily swayed, most especially when it is backed with prayers and strong spiritual foundation.

Stay interested and involved in what your teen is doing and continue to be aware of what he is up to. Be consistent with your message about your expectations. Even if your teen is influenced by their friends, you have clout, too. Teens often don't want to disappoint their parents, and often wait to try risky behaviour until they know what the consequences might be. Once your child reaches their teen years, lay out the rules and <u>consequences</u> for the activities they might be pressured into doing.

Build up your child's self-esteem and confidence
Children who have strong self-esteem are better at resisting negative peer pressure and influence.

You can <u>build your child's self-esteem and confidence</u> by encouraging her to try new things that give her a chance of success, and to keep trying even when things are hard. You can also be a role model for confidence too, and show your child how to act confident as the first step towards feeling confident. <u>Praising your child</u> for trying hard is important for building self-esteem and confidence.

I remember the story of a Pastor who shared a story of how his father has always threatened him because of his performance in school, and at times even beat him for performing very poorly. Then this term came and it was worse than expected. When his father was coming to pick him up from school, all that was running through his mind was what would happen between him and his father; when they were traveling back home, they were all silent in the car. Arriving home, he ran out to play with his friends and came back late; late at night the father called him to the sitting room and asked him whose son he is, and he responded to him. And the father told him, if he is really his son then he can do much better than this, he can make him proud. It was just a word, but that was the motivation that Pastor needed, and going back to school, his performance improved drastically.

Words are powerful and are triggers in determining what kind of self-esteem you want to build around your child.

Encourage a wide social network

If your child has the chance to develop friendships from many sources, including sport, family activities or clubs, it will mean he's got lots of other options and sources of support if a friendship goes wrong. As much as those avenues are beneficial to the child, they can equally be harmful, thereby calling for caution from your parents, so that it will not serve as another means where your child will build a serious negative influence.

There have been cases of girls connecting with people they have never met; but through these mediums they were either duped, raped, kidnapped or even killed. So parents must equally watch what activity they engage in on these kinds of networks.

Parents must stay interested and involved in what their teens are doing, and continue to be aware of what they are up to. They have to be consistent with their message about their expectations on whatever they intend to help their child avoid or stay away from, it is as simple as that.

PART FOUR

The Teacher, For Educational And Moral Child Upbringing

Chapter 12

The Teacher/Instructor/Guide

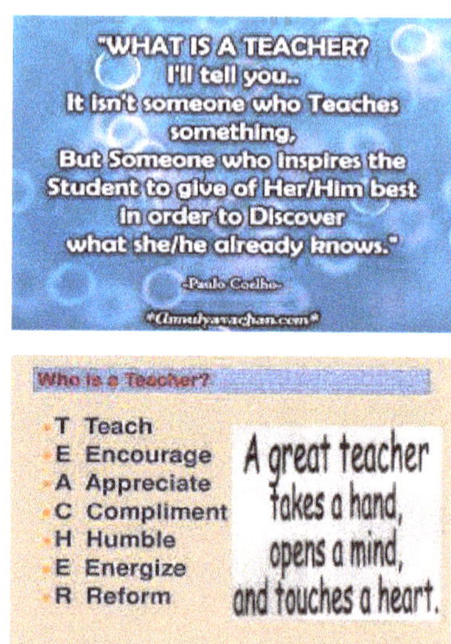

The role of a teacher in the life of a child cannot be over emphasized. But the teacher must know this, he/she serves as the intermediary between what a child could not learn at home to what he should learn at the place of learning, which can be the church, school, clubs and so on.

As a primary and secondary school teacher, you have at least 5 hours in a week that you spend with a child, while for those in the higher institutions a minimum of 2 hours that you spend with them. However, for someone who teaches in the Sunday Schools, he/she has just a maximum of 2-3 hours every week; but the expectation parents have in such a person is higher. I recalled in my second year as a Sunday School Teacher, we had this Chaplain in the school who really encouraged Sunday School activities for the first time. During that year's Sunday School day celebration, as was normally done by the Church, he said and I quote "at the end of every week, parents will send all their children to be taught under one person/teacher, some are having good manners and others do not and these teachers shout and talk for hours till their voices sometimes go off. Most times, parents are eager for another Sunday to come so that they can quickly send them (the children) to Church so they can have some peace. These teachers are really doing their best and are not being appreciated most times. They are the real heroes who never had the time to be celebrated, because they hide in a corner and keep molding these children that are not biologically their own the best way they can, God bless them".

A **teacher** (also called a **school teacher** or, in some contexts, an **educator**) is a person who helps students to acquire knowledge, competence or virtue.

Informally the role of teacher may be taken on by anyone (e.g. when showing a colleague how to perform a specific task). In some countries, teaching young people of school age may be carried out in an informal setting, such as within the family (homeschooling), rather than in a formal setting such as a school or college. Some other professions may involve a significant amount of teaching (e.g. youth worker, pastor).

In most countries, *formal* teaching of students is usually carried out by paid professional teachers. This article focuses on those who are *employed*, as their main role, to teach others in a *formal* education context, such as at a school or other place of *initial* formal education or training.

A **teacher** is a person who helps people to learn. A teacher often works in a classroom. There are many different kinds of teachers. Some teachers teach young children in kindergarten or primary schools. Others teach older children in middle, junior high and high schools. Some teachers teach adults in more advanced schools (for example, colleges and universities). Some are called professors.

There are different ways of teaching. Most teachers use a variety of methods to teach. Teachers often explain new knowledge, write on a blackboard or whiteboard, sit behind their desks on chairs, help students with their work, or mark students' work. They may use a computer to write tests, assignments or report cards for the class.

In my own opinion, the teacher is a person who bridges the gap of parenting in the life of a child, so that what the child feels is missing in his life or family, he/she finds the completion in the life of a teacher.

A teacher is not necessarily one who teachers in a class, or Sunday School or any place of meeting, a teacher is one who inspires, disciplines and fills a void. Teachers facilitate student learning, often in a school or academy or perhaps in another environment such as outdoors. So, I can say a teacher is someone a child submits to for guidance and proper upbringing.

A teacher's role may vary among cultures. Teachers may provide instruction in literacy and numeracy, craftsmanship or vocational training, the arts, religion, civics, community roles, or life skills.

Formal teaching tasks include preparing lessons according to agreed curricula, giving lessons, and assessing pupil progress.

A teacher's professional duties may extend beyond formal teaching. Outside of the classroom teachers may accompany students on field trips, supervise study halls, help with the organization of school functions, and serve as supervisors for extracurricular activities. In some education systems, teachers may be responsible for student discipline.

In many countries, a person who wishes to become a teacher must first obtain specified professional qualifications or credentials from a university or college. These professional qualifications may include the study of pedagogy, the science of teaching. Teachers, like other professionals, may have to or choose to continue their education after they qualify, a process known as continuing professional development.

Teachers are often required to undergo a course of initial education at a College of Education to ensure that they possess the necessary knowledge, competences and adhere to relevant codes of ethics.

Characteristics of a teacher

1. A teacher must be passionate
2. A teacher has to be tolerant
3. A teacher must be patient
4. A teacher must be loving
5. A teacher must be kind, and above all,
6. A teacher must be diligent

Let's read the stories of two individuals who have been unto the teaching line for a while, one teaches both in a school and the church.

The teacher is a nurse; he/she is always the first contact of the child in times of emergency at school or any meeting point.

He/she is a counsellor, the closeness of the teacher to the child can be shown through the kind of information the child opens up to the teacher which mostly deals with what the child is facing, either at home or treatment given to him/her when living with other people, or if the child has a bad behavior, the teacher equally fills the gap also and tries to give his/her own advice in such cases.

I never had plans of becoming a teacher, since my secondary school days. When I got into the university, I took accounting as a course, but when I later got married, I took in my first child, so I could not cope again.

Then I was inspired to go to the teaching line in the aspect of Physical Disability (after I did a change of course to Special Education), I wanted to teach in the disabled sector. What attracted me to that sector also was the sign languages used which I loved, but surprisingly I never learnt it at the tail end.

What caused all of these was seeing the pain and suffering our teachers were facing while in our Secondary School days; but I later enjoyed it after I joined the teaching line. I found out that it was much better as a woman and mother to teach, because it gives you time to be with your children and take care of them unlike other professions which hardly give you time for that. The teaching profession is more of half day and you are back home, and then you equally have holidays also which helps you to spend much time with your siblings, giving them the parental care and attention needed.

Later on, finding myself in the teaching line was really a thing of joy. With the experience I had, and the opportunity to relate with these young individuals and impact their lives the best way I can really, gives me peace and joy always.

Anonymous who shared her story also said, a teacher is someone that helps a learner, someone that takes the learner from the level of ignorance to the level of knowledge. A teacher must equally be able to take a child from the level of the unknown to the known. He/she brings out the best out of every child/student that comes his/he way in life. Without school or education, everyone would have been ignorant, there won't be technology and so on.

I had a passion for teaching and seeing people reaching or achieving their destiny because most professions you see today passed through the teaching line. When I see a child and teach him/her there is the tendency of him/her becoming a great person. So that passion has been there in me, that if a child becomes a great person tomorrow, I am fulfilled. So, aside from the passion, I see it as a calling from

God and have been teaching for over 38 years now; 28 in private and a proprietor since then.

Over the years, from my interaction with these students, I have seen a lot of positive results. I have received letters from those in the Primary and Secondary section which I was privileged to teach. Some after graduating and others sent theirs while still in school studying. I have equally received calls from some who appreciated my effort and where ever those I tutored see me, they always greet me; I still earn my respect from them. Another testimony came from one of them who presently lives in another state in the country, saying what he is today was as a result of the foundation he got (and that foundation always starts from the numbers and alphabets a child learns to the stage of knowing how to read and write).

Till date, if a child fails to perform as expected I become worried. Most times, this is because of the expectation I have on each of the children I tutored and still have on many of them, that at times makes me feel I have not done my work as I should have.

My advice to a teacher is be committed in your dealings with the child/student and not consider the amount you are to be paid in rendering your service; and to the government, they should motivate the teachers (most especially those working with them) by sending them for training to gain more experience and expertise, pay them as at when due to avoid any form of delay in them being committed to training the child also. They should stop nepotism and employ teachers who have the qualifications needed for every field.

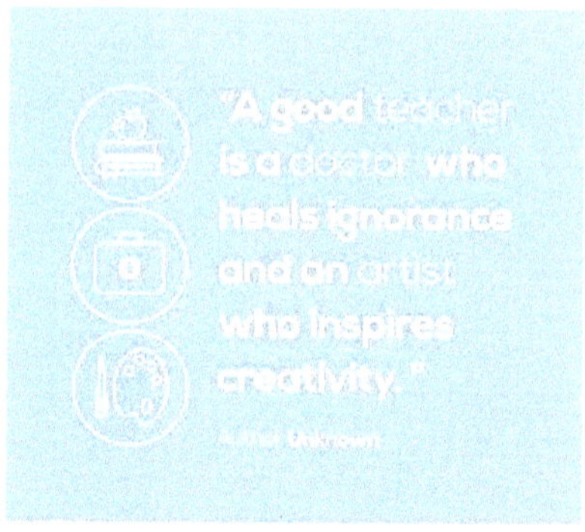

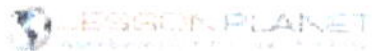

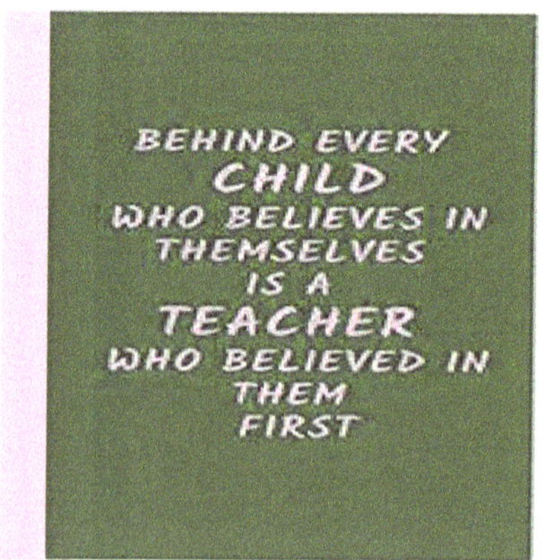

Broadly speaking, the function of teachers is to help students learn by imparting knowledge to them and by setting up a situation in which students can and will learn effectively. But teachers fill a complex set of roles, which vary from one society to another and from one educational level to another. Some of these roles are performed in the school and some in the community.

Inspires

Just a simple word like 'you can do it', 'I believe in you', keep pushing and so on can have a quick turnaround in the life of even a dull child, who is struggling to find his/her pathway in life, most especially in terms of education. The teacher in his entirety equally has other problems he/she needs to balance in life; but the moment it comes to inspiring his wards/students, it becomes so difficult for such a person to create this balance to achieve the required results in most cases. That's why you hear children saying 'Miss so and so forgot to say goodbye', Mr. so and so forgot to say, good job, well done". It might just be an ordinary word to an adult, but to a child, that means a lot to his development; such words create a level of belief and the desire to strive hard, in most cases to make the child proud and then his/or family. In as much as a child expects the immediate member of his/her family to equally be his inspiration towards success, most times the teacher is highly regarded. I recall when I was taking home lessons some years back, I came across this girl who has dyslexia, and I was meant to teach her. At first, I went with the normal thought of just flowing along, but I realized she was different, I did not know it was Dyslexia at first, so I easily got angry with her, because at her age, I thought she should comprehend faster and easier compared to a younger child, but reverse was the case. So I easily got angry because I had told her of my expectations of her, and she was not meeting up. Until I watched a movie that talked about a similar case with her own. On coming back, the next week, I knew I needed to take a different approach, instead of the normal teaching time, I now took more of my time engaging her in games and other activities that will help build her confidence and believe in herself; in no distant time she improved better than I expected (even though she later fell back again sadly, left the house where she was and got married). But at that very time, you could see that hope had risen. The same experience and the same estate, but this girl was different, all she needed was someone who would believe in herself and push her hard to make it through. After resuming school, her performance improved immensely; mind you the first girl was over a year and the second was a month. Some of them will always have a quick response to being inspired, and others might take time. So as a teacher, you must equally imbibe the habit of patience as you engage with these young ones.

A Spiritual lead/guide

As a spiritual guide or lead to a child, it is not when you carry your Bible or how conversant you are with the scripture. The way you approach certain situations tells what kind of guide you are. The Bible made it clear in Matthew 5:16 "**Now that I've put you there on a hill top, on a light stand – shine! Keep open house; be generous with your lives. By opening up to others, you'll prompt people to open up with God, this generous Father in heaven**" – **The Message,**

"Let your light shine before men in such a way that they may see your good works, and glorify your Father who is in heaven - New American Standard Bible. Which implies as a teacher, there are certain requirements set aside for you to live by, because in shaping or molding a child, they watch you closely than you think, and one wrong action or turn you take can demoralize that child, and since most of them cannot challenge you to your face, they remain broken, discouraged and without a direction. In most cases, when a child sees you as a guide and realizes you smoke, drink, go for clubbing, engage in sexual activities, and other things not worthy to be heard of, how do you expect that child to see you? Your life should be the mirror that this child should look at and see his/her replica any day and time.

As a teacher, in as much as the salary is equally important, there are other roles:

Disciplinarian

The Webster Dictionary defines a disciplinarian as a person who is very strict about punishing bad behavior. A person who uses discipline as a way of making sure that rules or orders are obeyed. Discipline is one of the key requirements that every teacher and instructor must possess. It forms the other parts of all that is needed in training and raising a child in the proper manner. Talking about discipline does not just include punishing the child when he/she is wrong, there are many ways you can go about that. As a teacher, your words, manner of approach, how jovial you are and so on is very important. Most times, you don't have to say a word to them (children), but how disciplined you are will show or tell, and in no time, you will notice these children want to always be around you. And over time, you build a level of trust that lasts long amidst them.

But as a teacher, if you are proud, use abusive words in addressing them, are mean and unapproachable, these children will find it difficult to be around you, they don't hate you or don't want to associate with you, but your behavior makes it difficult for them to be around you.

So, as a disciplinarian, you must be clear on your expectations. How do you want the child to respond to a question you ask, be reasonable, be consistent, use mistakes as opportunities to teach?

Teacher

As a teacher, your life entirely is a lesson to them. What you do and say, how you communicate and interact with them, are very key. So, as a teacher, you must always teach with every means possible to ensure that these young ones learn the best way they can, because you are working on a soul that tomorrow will represent you in a field you don't know of. So, you teach, you mold, direct and guide, encourage and assist where necessary for the right thing to be done or carried out. You might think you are ending up in the classroom, but the lives you have shaped in the right direction speaks of whether you were a good teacher or not.

Reformer

As a teacher, it is expected that any child that comes your way, must change positively. Most especially if the child was raised without manners at home, he must always go back looking different from who he is at home. It gives you credit and speaks a lot about your competence. As a reformer, you always look out for aspects in the child that you feel are not right and proper, and begin to work on it the best way you can. Maybe he/she might be a bully, stubborn, always using offensive words to hurt his peers or mates; but you need to find a way around it and make the child either stop using it completely, or reduce its use. There are behaviors that parents can accept at home, and to you as a teacher, you cannot and should not accept.

I was told of a child who at home beats his parents 'jokingly' and they respond also in that manner, but while in school, he is well behaved. That's because he knows his teacher will not tolerate that. It should reach the extent that when the parents threaten to inform you (the teacher) the child should show a level of remorse or be sorry for his action. Know that at this stage, you are not being mean or strict, you are trying to correct an aspect in his/her life that you feel is not right. At the moment, if care is not taken you will have serious issues, but insistence on the right thing to be done will later earn you respect and applause, it might be immediate or might be in the future.

Leader

As it is generally said, leaders lead by example. Back then in our secondary school days, we had teachers that drink, we equally have teachers that have really impacted our lives the best way they can. As a leader to these young ones, it is either you are leading them the right way or not, there are no two ways about that; but also know that whatever way you decide to lead them, there is a consequence for that action. you must equally be willing to make them become better in their day, achieving more than what you were able to achieve in your time. Leaders are never selfish and always look out for the improvement of themselves in the lives of their followers. Jesus was a teacher and a leader, in as much as he came to restore the world back to the father, he knew he will not stay forever. So, he had to train and raise others who will carry the mentality of the kingdom, thereby raising a breed of people with the same mindset. So, he called and raised the twelve, who in turn raised other people from the day of Pentecost till today so that all over the world, one of the most dominant religions is Christianity, which originated from few people who bought and believed in the mindset sold by the twelve. That is how a teacher is, he raises and cultures these young ones, working and believing that someday they will do the same to young ones who follow them. Let me quickly add that the most difficult role ever to aspire for on earth is to lead; because you might have to labor for long without seeing a fruit, but a consistent pattern with patience applied in years to come, will yield fruits.

So, if you are a teacher and leading in the direction, you don't have to give in to pressure all around you thinking it is not working, it might not be long from now that just a seed or student you trained will be the one who will make you ascend levels you have not thought of.

Agent of Change

Have you ever imagined as a teacher how you will feel being the reference point for both your colleagues and students? There has been a slogan that has been used among my people, the 'change begins with me' syndrome. If every teacher will know what influence he/she can have in the life of a child or student and work with it, perhaps we will not have a differentiation between an intelligent and unintelligent student, between those termed as performing students to those termed as under-performing students in the society. One of the things an agent of change looks out for always, is not how to use an opening he/she has to exploit or take advantage of those placed under his/her care, but to look out for opportunities and means of making the person better, stronger and equipped for the task ahead of that person.

Apostle Paul had the opportunity to have used Silas and Timothy to his own advantage, but throughout his journey, he always strengthens and encourages them, stressing on the need for them to be ambassadors of Christ and never allow anyone look down on them as youths, but be bold and stand strong against all odds or darts thrown at them.

Agents of change are not selfish, center focus, ambitious, greedy etc. But they are people who always think of how to encourage and improve someone to equally be better. Teachers must therefore be open to teach and instruct as well as guide all those God brought their way in all ramifications, first looking up to God for direction on how to impart the lives of these young ones positively.

Any time I am privileged to teach or instruct, all I see is an opportunity or opening to impart knowledge the best way I can to another person, some later appreciated learning under me, and others never had the chance to; but what gives me joy at the end of every engagement with them is the realization that they were taught something new, something that tomorrow they could equally apply and see it work for them as it has worked for me. I am not boasting about this, because I am not a qualified teacher when it comes to teaching and communication in a classroom setting, but as a Sunday School Teacher, I have some exposition in this regard at some point; but one thing that always stands out most for me is to know that those I taught or engaged are happy and could recall what was taught after that. That always gives me joy against any other thing, I might look tired and stressed at the end, but I will go home fulfilled knowing I have delivered the best way I can.

Judge of achievement

I had this C.R.S teacher back then in my Secondary school days, most of the students call her mum. Not because of any affiliation, but there is a way she interacts with her students, that the joy we have of being around her is great; she has a way of making you feel guilty when you are wrong or at fault. I could vividly recall one of those experiences. I did something bad to one of the staff, I was actually wrong but there was no evidence to prove I am suspect, so I decided to deny, because it was based on assumption. I was beaten but I refused to admit to my crime; I was even threatened by that staff but I was not moved. Other staff members even went on to call me names, but I insisted on one thing, what's your evidence and I will agree to it; as I was in front of the staff room, this teacher came and looked me straight in the eyes and said, Plangkat did you, do it? I looked at her boldly and said no, she asked the second time and I replied no, then she said 'let your yes be yes and your no be no' and she left. That was when I began to weep (but all those times I was being whipped, I was just crying so that the staff will allow me go), not because she whipped me, but just those words she said sank deep in my heart, and all I thought was, so someone still believes that this boy is innocent and is just being accused? I really wept until I was asked to go. That was how I improved in her subject until I came out with a good result in my SSCE that year, and I was proud I did

Parent substitute

I have heard of instances where a child leaves the house for school and never cares whether his parents say goodbye or not, whether you look good or not, but on one occasion, a teacher forgot to tell one of her students, your hair looks good. And for the whole of that day, the girl was moody and could not concentrate, it was towards the end of school that the teacher noticed she looked quite different from other days and decided to enquire what really was the problem, and the young girl said 'aunty, you forgot to touch and commend on my hair today', the teacher was surprised and had to quickly complement the girl and she was up and steady till the end of school that day. I also remember times that some of my students will offend parents at home, and then come and plead with me to please beg on their behalf, believing their parents will listen to me, and see that work as well. I remember another instance where a child did something wrong in front of the parent, and I just said 'don't do that again' and that child quickly stopped, and all the parent could say was 'but if it was me, he would not listen'.

My worry is, in time to come, it might be difficult for a parent to tell his/her child to stop and that child will do that obediently without saying 'are you my teacher'? Because the teacher seems to gain more respect for the biological parent of that child, the reason being that most parents are usually soft and gentle when it comes to the discipline and correction of the child, while the teacher is hard but with an understanding. In some cases, it might also be that, parents beat/discipline the child in anger and hardly get the chance to call the child and explain or tell the child what wrong he did that made them behave that way, while the teacher after whipping the child tells the child his/her fault which always brings about an understanding between them both.

I remember a time, one of the classes I took was Primary 5. On this day, they were making noise and I called those whom I saw, but they did not come. I went upstairs to their class, called them out and whipped them, then I left without saying a word at first, after I was sure the anger had subsided for both of us, then I called them and explained to them why I had to do what I did, guess what? The next day, we were playing as friends again.

As a teacher, you must always be open to these young ones. Some of them might be experiencing molestation, abuse and other acts that should not be, and the only person they can think of opening up to for help and direction or proper action to be taken is you. You might know of their sexual life and other secrets about them which their parents will never have the chance or the opportunity to know about, but that depends on how open you are to them, the listening ears you give to them, the attention you equally give to them and their needs as well, whenever they share or open up to you.

One other thing as a teacher you need to be very careful about is showing or giving special attention to particular children or students at the expense of others; it is very okay to commend and acknowledge those who are excellent and doing well, but they should not be given more attention as against the others. You must create a balance, so that the weak in the class will equally know that they have the hope to improve. In one of the classes I taught, I was the assistant in that class, so myself and the class teacher would call one weak and one strong student in the class, give special attention to the weak and less to the excellent or brilliant one. In this way, the brilliant will finish early and the weak are being guided towards completing the task they were asked to do. Over time, I noticed almost all the children of that class improved. A balance was created which helped the weak to cope. At some point I remember telling some of the students, you can do better than what you were doing now. I was not the most celebrated teacher that time, but I was one of the few these children were happy to be around. Even now that I no longer teach, whenever we meet, you can still see the friendship and love as it were in those days. Some opened up to issues that I had to give them guidance the best way I could, and the next day they came back happy and I knew it worked for them, some still came to say it never worked and after trying other methods they equally were happy thereafter.

Parents, even though a teacher is not permitted to influence your child to the extent that you do not have a say in his/her affairs (even though you always need to), if you fail to take your full responsibility as a parent should, then you have no other option than to permit that to take place, in some cases it might as well be for your own good, while in others it might lead to what can wreck your family apart. But the choice is all yours to make.

Confidant to students

The best examples I could think I have ever had for sometime were my teachers. There is this synergy I had with some of them during those years that have really helped my growth. To the extent that every day when going to school (in my Primary days), all I could always love school for was how they made us feel. In my Secondary school days, it was my principal (as well as few staff), there is a way he is fund of knowing each and every of his students; and the way he talks about his students outside, when you get to hear about it, it makes you want to do something to make him happy. Even though late now, one memory of his I have always remembered was when he told us to set his expectations of us as the seniors, he has a way of keeping a tap on us to ensure we get things done right. It made us build this level of confidence to do things that will make him happy. When he fell sick and left the school for treatment, it was a very sad moment for us. Upon his return months later, you could see the joy in the eyes of my set mates.

He built this confidence in us to believe in ourselves and our dreams and pursue it with all levels of seriousness. He was not just a teacher, but a mentor, an inspiration to a lot of us, and we will live to always remember him even in death.

Teachers, in building the confidence of your students, you don't use one method. A child might not perform according to your expectation in class, but there are other activities that when you engage him/her you get the required result, why not channel your energy in that direction also. Most teachers believe that as long as a child is not brilliant in class, he/she is dull; but learning and education generally does not end within the four corners of a classroom. One child might be excellent in class but in other aspects, the reverse is the case.

One major reason for us starting this initiative (G.M.I) was to encourage education and to expose these young ones to other areas that they can be good and excellent at. Over the years I realize that one should never under-estimate what a child can do based on what he could not do or the child not performing to your expectation elsewhere.

Challenges faced or experienced by teachers

Sexual Temptation: This occurs most often in settings where it is a single school (dominantly a girl's school), some of the male teachers will want to take advantage sexually of these young girls they were meant to help, thereby ruining their lives and career. Even though it happens in the boy's school, it's not paramount as it is in the girl's school.

Discouragement: Most of the teachers tend to be discouraged considering the effort they put to the work and what they are paid at the end. So, instead of most of them giving their time and dedication to the work, they tend to be unserious in handling activities that pertains to the life and development of the students.

Lack of exposure to trainings: In some cases, these teachers are not exposed to the current skills and training needed (both in the secular and religious sector) for them to perform the roles effectively in the training of these young ones. At the end, what parents consider and always say is that either the teacher is not serious or does not take his/her job seriously without looking at the loop holes and gaps making it difficult to give in their best.

Behavior of the child towards academics

This has become an issue to most teachers, when having a large class with children of different behaviors, it becomes a big issue to them; feelings of frustration, discouragement and in most cases the use of abusive words become common. While in the private setting, teachers have less to worry about. That is because there is a number that is needed per class which they try to maintain to enhance a better way of teaching, which also helps them to be able to cope with the behaviors from these children.

Frustration

Teachers have high expectations of the student/child, and once he/she is unable to meet up to that, frustration always steps in. In some cases, like the Government schools (L.E. As and G.S.S), most of the students find it difficult to comprehend, (cannot write their names or even read and write, so teachers have to begin to teach them from the beginning again) making it difficult for the teachers to give in their best (even though, not all the students have that problem, but most do). In most cases, teachers are being blamed for not taking their time in teaching these children, whereas in most cases, they might not have finished a syllable before moving into another class thereby affecting them intellectually and developmentally; these are aside strike actions carried by the teachers.

Lack of seriousness from the child

Unlike in the past where students worked hard to come out with good results in school, the present child/student is less concerned about his/her performance. As a result of their unserious nature, most of them now prefer to cheat in order to pass with excellent results. In such cases, the student/child will expect the teacher to come and assist him/her during examinations (Terminal, WAEC or NECO and so on). That in itself has been an issue for the teacher to try to cope with. In some cases, some teachers don't actually dedicate time to their work effectively.

When you teach a child and you later on ask questions and then ask questions and get a positive response from the students/child, as a teacher you always feel encouraged. But when reverse is the case, it is usually frustrating

Poverty level

In some other cases, most especially the government section (s), these children have already been introduced to the life of struggles due to the poverty line from a young age. So, in remote villages or areas, when it is farming season, you will hardly find students committed to academics, and most of these cases are being encouraged by parents. A teacher narrated the case of a child who was caught with drugs during school hours, after been interrogated, he confessed to taking it to have the strength to work at the mining site he goes to fend or work to cater for his immediate family needs, the mother was called to further make enquiries, and she admitted to the fact that the child is the breadwinner of the family. So, he uses weekends to go and work in the mining site and uses the weekdays for his studies (he confessed taking it because he saw that the drugs give the other workers strength to work)

Number of children in a class

In most of these government institutions, you find a class of about 80 or more students present under the supervision and control of one or at most two teachers. In such situations, a teacher cannot meet them individually (a good class setting is supposed to accommodate at most 30 students), thereby making it relatively difficult for the teacher to know the weakness of the child and where he or she needs help. Most times, at the end of a session you find out that the teachers find it difficult to know all the children by names and other areas of weakness which they are supposed to know and come to their aid.

Lack of materials and infrastructure

These are common with most of the Government institutions of learning. Lack of teaching materials to enhance his/her ability in terms of a good delivery in the place of teaching, making the teacher to go on personal research in cases whereby the needed materials are not provided or made available by the government, using their finance for those research purposes in order to ensure effective delivery to the child. Some teachers end up skipping such topics that need research (and might be important to the child) due to lack of adequate finance to carry on with that. While in terms of the infrastructure, most Government learning centers are not provided with the needed facilities to enable good teaching, you find that most of the structures are old and worn out, no comfortable places for the students to sit and learn and these are supposed to have been given the most priority against any other, but reverse tends to be the case, in my country. In such cases, it becomes very difficult for the student/child to assimilate whatever is being taught by the teacher, and that also is frustrating. But in the private section (s) this is not always experienced because of the ability of proprietors to ensure they meet the government regulations and standard for education.

Finance

This is mostly experienced by those in the private sector. Difficulty to access funds in order to add more structures to the existing ones so as to aid effective teaching as it should, and to equally pay the staff employed so that they can give in their best to teaching and imparting the lives of these young ones as it should be.

Inability of parents to pay fees

This is experienced by both the government and private sectors (though not all from the private sector but most from the government). Parents who know the value and worth of education will always go to any length to see that their children are well educated and knowledgeable; and perhaps those who fail to see from that angle might be due to the fact that they were not opportune to go to school; whether parents, guardians or even step-parents. So, it has become a stigma, that even if the child does not go far they ask themselves; what do I have to lose? Or there are other 'things the child can do to make a living aside from schooling' so I don't have to pay as at when needed, so when I have, I will settle the debts. But most forget that this thought is dangerous, with the trend in which the world is moving, the least a child should be able to acquire is primary education, and once he/she is denied that it becomes an issue. Also, with education, he or she can associate with his/her peers comfortably and lack of that makes his/her peers have a hedge over him/her. Other challenges are:

1. Tax and levies from the government
2. Ability of some students/children to comprehend as expected
3. Lack of permanent/consistent teachers

What's the way out?

Unlike in the private institutions, for that of the public institution, they seem to almost have lost hope for any improvement at the moment. Looking at a critical example, most of these Government Institutions mentioned are situated around the rural areas, while the private Institutions are mostly found in the rural-rural and urban-rural settings. Here are possible solutions that could be of help to both sectors:

Reduction of the poverty level

If the poverty level of parents in these remote areas can be improved through providing scholarships for these children, as a way of curtailing any excuse of going to farm, trade or any other activity that will take the child's mind off school at that particular time, that will go a long way.

Awareness to parents

This has to be the sole responsibility of the government if they really want to help in raising a generation of children who will actually take over the helm of affairs and work towards the development of the child. So, when parents are enlightened on what is expected of them by the Government towards raising the child well, they will equally apply it in the lives of their children for effective growth. As well as making the work of the teacher lightened at last too.

The teacher's attitude towards teaching and communication

Once the head decides to do the right thing, the whole-body parts follow suit. That's who a teacher is, he/she is the head outside the home, once he/she aligns and decides to do the right thing, the students equally adapt to the new change. This includes insistence on no malpractice, which some teachers are involved in, while in some cases the external body conducting the exams too is equally a part of. So, for a teacher who is not serious, he/she has to become serious in ensuring that he/she delivers as much as is expected of him/her and at the particular time.

So, students must change their attitude towards learning, teachers must change their attitude towards teaching and parents must change their attitude in communicating with the child; and all of these circles around effective communication.

Teachers should not always be blamed when a child fails to perform as expected by the parents. Parents and the teachers all have a role to play when it comes to the development of the child. Parents have a way of thinking that the teacher should pay more attention to their child forgetting that in the place of learning, a teacher is supposed to give equal attention to all the children under his/her care.

In some other cases, some parents engage the services of househelps and do not give them the needed care as they should, some of them do not sleep well, and do not eat a balanced diet food, and with all of this, such a child is still expected to be in the school the next day. In such a pitiful situation, if such a child is still determined to learn and excel, he/she will still push hard with determination and focus as well as resilience, he/she will make it through. Inasmuch as all of these factors matter and are key, it also rallies around the child, and the teacher; teaching well as it is expected.

Finance

There should be institutions who should be willing to step in to provide loans or assistance to schools where necessary. This is to help them in having more facilities and structures to aid teaching and create a conducive environment for the students/child.

Motivation to teachers

Take an instance with those in the private sectors, if proprietors could provide allowances and other incentives (that is, to schools who are not doing that) to the teachers, it encourages them and helps them to be committed to their services and give in their very best also as expected.

Core values

Either in the private or government institutions, there should be objectives, values and conditions guiding a teacher on what is expected of him. Take for instance in cases of molestation, when such laws are put in place, it helps the student to study knowing he/she will not face such harassment from the teacher. In the case of such occurrences, his/her appointment is terminated to serve as a warning to other staff/teachers who indulge in such acts or behaviors.

I started my teaching career (as a Sunday School teacher) in the year 2010, when I was still a student. As a student in SS1, I had both class, hostel and individual responsibilities that I needed to meet up with. And if I don't do all of that, especially the first two, it would always lead me into trouble with seniors. There were these two seniors in SS2 at that time who were already Teachers, so I decided to just join as a way of staying out of those activities since the football I loved, I was not encouraged in. After joining, the next term we were asked to ensure we join the different Sunday School Departments during holidays, because when we return in the next term, we'll be given responsibilities to handle. I was scared and did not want anything that would bring about disgrace to me, so during the holiday I decided to join through the help of one of my teachers in the Sunday school who has always been an inspiration. That was my journey into becoming a teacher.

During those years, I noticed that a child in its entirety is another world of learning for whoever intends to learn. Then after my graduation two years later, I decided to take a teaching job, at first also, it was because as a graduate I lacked a job and admission was yet to come and I cannot stay at home 'idly", so the best option was to teach. The salary was actually small, but over time I realized that the salary I was paid was not as important as the time I had with the students, and their openness to learn whatever as a teacher I am willing to teach them. I had to make them my close friends the best way I could, so that salary was not important to me compared to what I can see these children learning, and what they can be exposed to, to make them grow to become better people. My drive became what I could add in the lives of these young minds like myself to see that they equally make it and in the right manner. So, I had double areas where I always engaged with them, in the Church where I was a teacher and in the School where I am a teacher.

It is 12 years now and still counting, but over the years I realize that my major motivation was to see that they become better, if possible, than I am. At one point in time, I recalled telling them that they need to work as hard as they can to become great, because I will equally be great, and when great people meet, they discuss ideas, all to spur them to have a positive mindset of greatness. I am happy and proud today when I see most of them and what has become of them. Then in 2013, to further drive the course of helping raise a child, we started an initiative. It was just a gathering of friends, and the aim was to equally spur them towards believing in themselves, knowing they are great and God has a plan for each and every one of them, and channeling their thoughts towards positive thinking. It just used to be a meeting within the Church Premises, until 2016 when the need came for expansion so that people from other Churches can equally join to benefit from the programs, then we had our name G.M.I (Great Minds Initiative), with one aim raising them as models who will model the next generation and having a continuity in that regard. Over the years, even though still young, I have equally watched them grow, all of them striving at their different ends towards the same goal and vision established over the years; and am yet to be proud until all of them strive hard to reach that level and position designed by God for each and every one of them.

I love working and being around them (children) as a teacher, because it has helped increase my thinking capacity, it helped me know that there is no better people one can always be around like them, because you will always see their willingness to know, asking questions and just eager to know that they are loved and have the attention they need. As a teacher, you have the opportunity to shape the child to the desired position you want.

That is my own experience and what inspired me over the years to help them believe in themselves against all odds, until they break through to become who God has planned for them to be. The role of a teacher cannot be over emphasized, be it in a secular or religious setting, remember to give in your best for the sake of that child and the parents who entrust them in your care.

Reading through this chapter, you will find that it speaks about the teacher from the religious and secular perspectives, but stresses more on the secular part of teaching. This is because of the constant engagement these teachers have with the children, which gives them more room to channel their strength towards the development of the child.

So, the secular teacher works on the educational, physical, psychological development of the child, while the religious teacher works on the spiritual and emotional development of the child. In engaging with the child, it doesn't really matter about the setting of the meeting as much as what the child gets to learn, what value he/she tends to grow up with towards becoming a better person. As a teacher or tutor (most especially in the secular part), research is very key to your communication with a child, every time the teacher will engage the child, he/she should have been prepared for that, and the only way is through research. Through those researches carried out, it widens the horizontal scope of the teacher when communicating with his/her students.

As a parent, you are equally a teacher either to your children or others. And if the way you train and raise your child cannot be replicated in another child's life, then you have failed in the responsibility of being a teacher. Teaching is multi–dimensional and should not be viewed from one angle or conclude that it is not possible to try other methods. We must equally abuse the statement that says "the reward of teachers is in heaven", if their reward is in heaven, should they be given stipends to manage at the expense of their well-being? If today, all the teachers decide to say they will no longer commit to teaching, will there be another generation that will rise to be knowledgeable? Countries and Governments must realize that all professions existing on earth went through all these teachers, that most people are finding it difficult to respect in our present-day society, (even though some teachers actually ruined some of their students and made them become what they are today).

As a teacher, inasmuch as it is advised you go for further studies, you equally should know that you cannot know everything at the same time. Most times, these children will want to approach you with questions or suggestions they feel is helpful to both you and them for easier communication. Your ability to allow yourself to be teachable at such moments is very important.

I watched a movie sometime back (an Indian movie) called Chalk and Duster. It was all about teachers in a school who became fond of their students, but over time there was a change in the management of the school, making life take a U-turn to the teachers. Some were asked to resign and others had to bear the pains irrespective of not being convenient with what was happening. One of the teachers later fell ill as a result of the treatment from the school head at that time and was asked to resign, calling her teaching method outdated, and it became a national issue; that was when the students she trained in the past using the method rose to her defense, and the hospital she was admitted was being managed by one of her students. Later on a national broadcast was sponsored whereby a questions and answers session was conducted for two of the staff who tried to go against the management. If they could answer all the questions correctly, they would not only win a cash prize but would equally be reinstated as teachers. It all turned out in their favor, but one thing was learnt in the course of time, children and students began to learn to respect their teachers. It was just a movie, but that was supposed to be the replica of what should have been happening in our society, whereby when a teacher is paid, the government and proprietors will not think it is a favor they are doing to the staff, but that they are equally co-proprietors working as a team to see to the well-being and development of a child. When that is done, then all those who were taught by these staff, teachers or lecturers, should equally remember to say thank you. When that is done, even though the reward of a teacher is in heaven, he/she also sees some of the benefits while on earth.

To the teachers, always remember you are the second parent a child has, when you fill the void properly, you raise a leader and your replica. But the thing is, whichever way you decide to take, always remember to ask yourself one question, what will I choose to be remembered for by the students I taught, trained, raised and cultured? When you train them in the right way you always raise your head proudly when referring to them as your students, but when you do not, you will always bow your head in shame knowing you never gave them the best they needed as your students.

We have a popular saying, boldly written inside the Assembly Hall of my secondary school, which says 'whatever a man sows, that must he reap'. Then I ask you as a teacher, what are you sowing in the lives of these young wards/children placed under your care by their parents? And what will you reap at the end of their maturity?

Conclusion

Children and youths should be flexible, humble and have a listening ear for their parents and other older folks, because they have also passed through the same developmental stages in their early stages and have key lessons or experiences which could be helpful and impactful as well. Running away from blame will not solve the situation, neither will accusation, and fundamentally such parental advice and experience comes through the use of the word of God as ordained in the Bible.

Together, both the younger and older generation can bridge the generation gap and move forward in order to overcome the challenges of our time as well as become bridge builders for the generation coming next.

Three key institutions that shape a child are: the home, the church or other religious background and the school. Children are served best when all three institutions point them in the same direction. Only an education that has the liberty to address the whole child – socially, intellectually, emotionally, physically and spiritually reaches the possibility of excellence.

If your child is on the right path because of your effort in training him/her, it makes you happy and proud, but if they are on the wrong path, it makes you sad. It now becomes your responsibility to train your child to do what is good in the home, church and other religious setting, school and society so that you will be proud of them and enjoy peace in your later years. I feel the same, because the child will always tell people that it is my parents that helped me become what I am today. So, if you help your child do the right thing, they will one day commend you.

Roberts Liardon wrote in his book *Run to the Battle*, "No longer will children be nice little boys and girls who play with toys that you buy, but they shall be children who pray, sing and do the work of the Lord while they are yet young, when you train them." (Roberts Liardon, 1989)

How are you training your children? Is it in the way of the Lord? Be encouraged that it will not go in vain. Are you plagued with guilt because your children are wayward? Trust God, he will help you correct your mistakes and start all over again. Make an honest assessment of why your child/children are wayward. If you have been negligent, confess to God and seek His help, He will give you what is needed to help your wayward child/children. So, do not give up on the wayward child, but keep praying and remember the story of the prodigal son (Luke 15:11-32), which I believe will help you persevere in prayer.

Training a child prepares him/her to live in the world and be responsible. Training a child proves that parents love their children. When you discipline a child there is life and hope for the family and next generation, because the Bible describes children as a gracious gift from God, a heritage and reward from God as a crown and glory of old men (Psalms 127:3). They are God-given blessing and a responsibility, do not rob your children of the best way of training which is in God's way, it's in your hands as Joshua stated, 'but as for me and my house we will serve the Lord'.

Children need to be able to look to their parents as examples of the kind of people they want to be. So, parents, are you examples to your children?

Our present generation has a lot of effects and influence on the child, both negatively and positively.

A child can watch television for helpful and important Bant issues and information etc. Eruption of technologies, e.g., phones, access to internet, gadgets etc. are forms in which the child learns and gets educated mentally, physically, emotionally, educationally, spiritually, socially, psychology and so on, as well as can detain/stop the child from benefiting positively if not careful.

Parents are not to stop their children/child from possessing them, but are to be careful in the way they handle such things as well as monitor their usage of those things, so as to affect its negative effect on them as children.

Furthermore, the usage of these gadgets and technology implements should help the child build himself/herself and not make the child become a nuisance/trouble to you as parent and the society as a whole. So, it is your duty at most to check your child's activity with such things, making sure that he/she uses it the right way.

Where have you also refused to heed the warning or correction of your child? Jesus began teaching when He was still a child; Samuel was a child when God gave him warning to Priest Eli and his family, you might also be wrong without noticing that you are. If God can use these people and more, what makes you think He can't use your child? God uses even the child to speak forth His Word and commands, so using them to talk and warn you should not be something to feel offended about, but you should accept that you are being corrected/warned of with joy and satisfaction; so, when the child sees you learning from your mistakes, he/she learns from his/her easily.

The late singer/author Madame Ernestine Schumann Heink struck a responsive chord with all when she wrote these profound words *'home is the first school and the first church for young ones, where they learn what is right, what is good and what is kind, where they go for comfort when they are hurt or sick, where joy is shared and sorrow is eased. Where fathers and mothers are respected and loved, where children are wanted, where the simplest food is good enough for kings because it is earned. Where money is not so important as loving-kindness, where even the tea kettle sings from happiness. That is the home, God bless it'.* (Zig Ziglar, 2001). So, can your home be described like this?

A poem written by an unknown author titled **"Deepen and Sweeten your Relationship with your Child"** goes,

"Raise children to unfold the uniqueness in their hearts,

Teach children the true meaning of discipline

So, they can make life-affirming choices on their own

Help children see into others character

So, they can recognize those who bring out the best in them versus those who intend them harm

Raise children into mature adults who know their strengths

And use them to create a life of meaning and fulfilment"

Remember that when parents teach their children in God's way, they will be honouring God and he will reward them at the end.

The story of Rebekah and Jacob is a good example when speaking about communication in the family. When she was pregnant with the twins, she vividly recalled the words of prophecy she received about them "and the Lord told her, the sons in your womb will become two rival nations. One nation will be stronger than the other; the descendants of your older son will serve the descendants of your younger son." – Genesis 25:23.

She could vividly remember these words, which made the interaction between her and Jacob become very strong, making it difficult for the father to even stand between that promise even though he had tried hard to reverse the promise – Genesis 27:1-4. I am not saying the manner in which she took to make the promises of God come to pass was proper, but it also led to the fulfilment of it. To the extent that she suggested to the father for Jacob to go and live with her brother Laban so as to avoid bloodshed. Communication is very paramount to the growth of a child and the family, and looking at the context we are now talking about, once there is a gap in it, children almost always avoid any conversation with their parents, especially when in relationship with the other sex, and then pregnancy. But when there is a flow in communication, it makes it easier for the child to open up to the mother/father informing him/her of any development which has led to her being pregnant – i.e. for the girl.

The issues discussed in this book are not faced or experienced by a part of the world but it is a global issue that needs a wakeup call to parental responsibilities. Each parent must know that they should rise to those responsibilities to avoid havoc in the family and society at large. Parents therefore have to be up and running doing everything at all cost to see the effective growth of their individual families.

It is a fact as the popular saying goes "you give birth to a child but you don't give birth to their personality, you only help shape it". Children find it very difficult to understand that sometimes as a parent you are going those extra miles for them because you want the best for them. These are just a few to mention. These children easily learn to associate with the right company later on, knowing that their peers are people who will accept them just the way they are without condemning them. When this gradually happens, it begins to take the relationship which the child is supposed to have with their parents and they then become the comfort zone. And if the child is unfortunate to get the wrong peers, then it is obvious that the child will get ruined.

Parents need to know that the closer they are with their children the closer relationship they will have with them. Studies should not and cannot be a barrier between children and parents at any level of their development though the child has to study well and become better representatives in the society. At the same time the child needs more of the parents to build their confidence in becoming the person they would want to be in life.

Parents have the responsibility of helping their children find their own value in life. Values are things that we consider important, most children while growing up consider-possessions, popularity, fame, positions, instant pleasure, money, education as ultimate value. For them to get these things the most in life, parents must rather teach the children through example to embrace biblical based values such as good reputation, obedience to God, seeking to glorify God in all aspects of life, helping others and God's work etc. Most at times, children tend to pursue the wrong ambitions for certain feats, so that they could be seen, heard, and be praised by men.

In the month of March, we undertook a discussion on the teenage challenges with some teens in one of the units of the Church I work with. It's amazing some of the truths these young boys and girls shared, and amazingly most parents are not aware of it; so they live in an insecure world with unanswered questions not knowing who to open up to or share with. Thankfully to God, we were able to share some experiences we (alongside other adult members) shared during our teenage years with them, and you could see the smiles on their faces, because we made it an open discussion that we intend to help them through the stage. If as parents, you are able to understand every developmental processes of your child and show your intention and need to be part of it, they will always be willing to share, but the moment you show or give a sign of "that bothers you not me" mentality, they create a distance that over time leaves you in regret when it's late for you to make amends.

Your child of the kindergarten and primary school will not be the same as him or her at the secondary level or high school, and neither will it be the same with that of the tertiary level. Each of these stages has its peculiar challenges and problems, and the method of handling them differs in all these stages. So your ability to know which of them to apply automatically draws the child closer to you.

The teacher on the other hand, works hand in hand with the parents to help these children in these different processes, because he or she is the second parent that sacrifice most of his/her time with the child, though our system attaches one teacher to about 25 or more students in a class making it a bit difficult for him or her to know each child and his or her need, but as much as they do their best, it is left for the parent to augment the effort of the teacher.

If every unit that is involved in the raising of a child takes its role seriously as it should be, then I believe that almost all the problems of societal ills faced now will be eradicated, and the better world which we believe starts with each and every one of us will become a dream come true.

I might not be a parent yet, but someday I surely will be one. But these years of working with the children have opened me to a certain level of knowing about what parenting entails, and I am glad it did so I could share information that could be of great help to our bedeviled societies at large and to grieved or affected families. Let me conclude with this question to ponder on then, what will take your time and attention from your family, which is your first God given responsibility?

References/Glossary

1. Adapted from materials provided by Mentoring Partnership of Long Island, Virginia Mentoring Partnership, and the Big Brothers Big Sisters of America, Child Development Seminar, August 1990.

2. Adolescent Pregnancy: World Health Organization – WHO

3. Be a model worthy of Emulation: Fela Durotoye

4. Bible Study Fellowship (BSF), copyright © 1960, 2004, 2013

5. Broken vows and the next generation: Recognizing and helping when parental divorce is a spiritual trauma: Annette Mahoney, Heidi Warner, and Elizabeth Krumei

6. Caring for Children with Special Needs: THE AMERICANS WITH DISABILITIES ACT AND CHILD CARE

7. Dr. Harold J Sala. Train up a Child and be Glad You Did. Oasis International Limited, copyright © 1978 by Accent – B/P Publication

8. FAO Corporate Document Repository, produced by Forestry Department: titled, Community forestry herders decision-making in natural resource making management…

9. From the Devotional, When Motherhood Feels Too Hard

10. How Peer Pressure Influences Addiction: By Elizabeth Hartney, BSc., MSc., MA, PhD; Medically reviewed by Steven Gans, MD

11. How to Survive Teen Peer Pressure: By Barbara Poncelet, Updated on January 30, 2020

12. Human trafficking: Project Rahab Awareness Training Manual (PRATM) – Ven Lannap and Julbyen Lar

13. Jochebed: The Mother of Moses- John Phillips

14. Lessons from Esther: Mordecai Never Grew Weary by Mark Schindler Forerunner, April 1999

15. Oxford Advanced Learners Dictionary

16. Parenting a Child with a Disability: TIPS AND RESOURCES FROM JOURNEYS IN DISABILITY*

17. Parenting a Child with Special Needs: A publication of the National Information Center for Children and Youth with Disabilities - ND20, 3rd Edition, 2003

18. Paul Tripp's video, <u>Mirror of Sin & Means of Grace: Parents are Works in Progress Too</u>

19. Perry Stone. Breaking the Jewish Code, Copyright © 2009

20. Pictures/Images gotten from the internet

21. Poem by Shelley R. Davis, "Raising Children"

22. Poem by an Unknown Author, Deepen and Sweeten your Relationship with your Child

23. Roberts Liardon. Run to the Battle, copyright © 1989 by Albury Publishing

24. Scripture quotation marked AMP are taken from the Amplified Bible.

25. Scripture quotation marked NIV are taken from the New International Version, copyright © 1973, 1978, 1984 by International Bible Society

26. Scripture quotation marked GNV are taken from the Good News Bible, copyright © 1966, 1971, 1976, 1984 by photo offset process at Swapna Printing Work PVT Ltd, Kolkata

27. Social indicators and effects of marriage divorce in African societies

    Love Obiani Arugu, Department of Political Science and Strategic Studies; Federal University Otuoke, Bayelsa State, Nigeria

28. The Child with a Disability: Parental Acceptance, Management and Coping: The Scientific World

JOURNAL, (2007) 7, 1799–1809 TSW Child Health & Human Development

29. The Story of Joseph: All about the famous biblical dreamer who inspired a musical. By Elana Roth

30. The story of a young girl who became a mum when she was still a teenager: Birth Global Administrator | July 22, 2015

31. The Strong Character of Samson's Mother

32. Unplanned Journey of Parenting a Child with Special Needs: PARIPEX - INDIAN JOURNAL OF RESEARCH

33. "When Mothers Pray"– Duncan William

34. Wikipedia

35. Who is a parent? Bedford Borough Council

36. Zig Ziglar. You Can Reach the Top, copyright © 2001, by Zig Ziglar.

Ingram Content Group UK Ltd.
Milton Keynes UK
UKHW020149240323
419060UK00010B/256